FINAL SCORE!

FINAL SCORE!

IN THE HUDDLE

DAN FARR

TATE PUBLISHING
AND ENTERPRISES, LLC

Published by Tate Publishing & Enterprises, LLC
127 E. Trade Center Terrace | Mustang, Oklahoma 73064 USA
1.888.361.9473 | www.tatepublishing.com

Tate Publishing is committed to excellence in the publishing industry. The company reflects the philosophy established by the founders, based on Psalm 68:11,
"The Lord gave the word and great was the company of those who published it."

Book design copyright © 2014 by Tate Publishing, LLC. All rights reserved.
Cover design by Allen Jomoc
Interior design by Jimmy Sevilleno

Published in the United States of America

ISBN: 978-1-63268-966-5
1. Sports & Recreation/Football
2. Religion/General
14.07.31

To my best friend and wonderful wife, Becca, and to our daughters, Allison and Jillian. This book is in memory of my father, Lester E. Farr Sr., my mother, Allene Farr, and my father-in-law, Damon Ray.

CONTENTS

INTRODUCTION

Do you know a young person (or an adult) who is crazy about sports but you can't seem to get through to them about their need for Christ? I was once that person, and God used sports at the age of forty-eight to get me to see what Christ had done on the cross for me. This book is designed to help you break through the barrier.

Through this collection of devotions and short stories, I have attempted to combine my knowledge of sports, my growing knowledge of the Bible, and everyday experiences to connect the reader to the Gospel in a fresh, new way. Hopefully one of these stories will reach a young man or young woman for Christ who otherwise might have never known him.

Everyone needs to understand that it is very cool to know Jesus and for him to know us. Jesus taught the people two thousand years ago using ordinary stories about farming, water, marriage, and everyday life called parables. If Jesus wrote parables today, undoubtedly, he would toss in a few sports stories since so many people today are passionate about sports. The Apostle Paul shared with the Corinthians in 1 Corinthians 9:22, "Whatever a person is like, I try to find common ground with him, so that he will let me tell him about Christ, and let Christ save him." My hope and prayer is to share these sports-related parables in a way that the light bulb will come on for you to enable you to look at the cross as you never have before and allow God to change you and disciple you. To God be all the glory that might result from this book.

TESTIMONY

I am honored and privileged to share my testimony with you. On a Sunday morning in the late 1960s in a small Methodist church in middle Georgia, I could have received Christ. I was drawn to Jesus Christ by the Holy Spirit during a message by a lay speaker, but I was afraid of what people would say if I went to the altar. I escaped into the warm sunshine and convinced myself that I would have enough nerve to accept Christ the following Sunday. But I went back into the wilderness for thirty-five years. I did not attend church when I moved to Atlanta, but I met my future wife, Becca, through the sports ministry at Peachtree Presbyterian Church. We married the following year and were later blessed with two beautiful daughters, Allison and Jillian. We visited Mt. Zion UMC in East Cobb, which had a new gym. Two years later, I started a basketball program and poured my energy into it for the next twelve years. It was great seeing the program grow and packing the sanctuary on basketball Sunday. But my focus was too much about personal achievement and not enough about helping young people know Christ.

I continued to live a self-centered life and could go for days without communicating with God. But in 2001, I watched the ESPN Classic special about basketball star Pete Maravich, my idol throughout high school, college, and adulthood. My vintage Maravich jersey hung in my closet for twenty-five years. I bought throwback jerseys, books, and videos on eBay. One VHS tape was Pete's testimony that I watched one Sunday night out of boredom and curiosity. That video was a divine appointment. At the time, I was drifting away from the basketball program and was very unhappy with myself. I was so far from God after many years of living without him. Jesus on the cross? It was just a story until I heard Pete tell how Christ transformed him. I always wanted to be like Pete, but I realized I wasn't because Jesus Christ knew Pete Maravich, and Jesus didn't know me. Occasionally, I wondered during sermons, Am I going to heaven? Then I would fool myself by falling back on my good works. But I knew that if I died that evening, I would never see Jesus face to face. I cried out in my heart that I wanted my life to change. As my former pastor, Steve Lyle, often said, "It's not the words you pray as much as the attitude of your heart."

God has blessed me with many opportunities to share my testimony. At first, I was sure I had it all figured out, but instead, there was so much to learn. God led me to turn that basketball program into our Christ-centered Hoops2Heaven ministry. I eventually allowed him to change me in the workplace when I went through trying times after a merger. An opportunity came to teach high school Sunday school and lead the basketball ministry again, which led to the start of a year-round youth sports ministry at Mt. Zion. Can you see a pattern? Youth sports ministry is my fishing hole. I continue to pray that I can get it right for Christ for our families at Mt. Zion and in our community. God loved me unconditionally, wooed me, and showed me mercy time after time until I repented, which means that I turned from my sinful ways, trusted, and obeyed. Repent, trust, and obey. There is no other way. I'm far from perfect, but God thinks I'm worth it. I was lost and then found and forgiven.

FB01:
THE BLIND SIDE REVISITED

MATTHEW 25:40, MARK 12:30-31, JOHN 15:12, 1 JOHN 3:17

This is my commandment, that you love one another, as I have loved you.

—John 15:12

Becca and I saw a tremendous secular sports movie that also made a strong statement for Christ: The Blind Side. It stars Oscar-winner Sandra Bullock, who portrays Leigh Anne Tuohy, the wife of Sean Tuohy, a former Ole Miss basketball star. Leigh Anne's character is the perfect blend of Southern beauty, charm, street smarts, toughness, and compassion. The Blind Side is the true story of Michael Oher, a young man who was abandoned at birth by his father and at age seven by his mother in the toughest drug-infested section of Memphis. Michael gets a chance to attend a prestigious Christian school because of his size and athletic potential. Michael is eventually befriended and adopted by the Tuohys and becomes an All-American tackle at Ole Miss and a first-round draft choice of the Baltimore Ravens.

There are many poignant, heartwarming, compassionate scenes, but none more so than when Leigh Anne and Sean see him for the first time. Their son, S. J., and daughter, Collins, recognize him from school, and S. J. says, "That's Big Mike!" Big Mike is walking down the street in freezing weather in shorts and a tattered golf shirt. Leigh Anne tells Sean to roll down the window of their luxury SUV, and she asks him if he needs a ride home. He assures them that he is fine, and they drive past him.

That's where the leading of the Holy Spirit kicks in. You can sense Leigh Anne's struggle as her brain processes the facts: *Cold night, no car, no jacket, by himself. What will happen if I help this very large African American boy?* Suddenly, Leigh Anne shouts to Sean, "Turn around!" Sean makes a U-turn, and they pick up Michael, take him to their home, and let him sleep overnight on the downstairs sofa.

Leigh Anne wore a beautiful diamond cross necklace through-out the movie. But that cross wouldn't have meant much if she had ignored the calling of the Holy Spirit to help this boy in need. Too often, I have an opportunity to help someone in need but I ask myself, How will this impact me? Often, I commit a sin when I pass by putting my selfish needs ahead of others and the calling of Christ to help those in need. When I put my comfort ahead of others, I display my blind side to the world. My light doesn't shine for others to see his love. When Leigh Anne turned that car around, her Christian love shone brighter than her diamond cross.

Later in the movie, a friend remarks to Leigh Anne about how much Michael has changed. Actually, it is his circumstances that changed because Michael has a home, a family, three square meals a day, clothes on his back, and a great chance to earn a college scholarship. But he is still the same sweet Michael. Leigh Anne firmly replies, "He has changed me." When we reach out to others in the name of Christ, we find ourselves changed to be more like Christ.

Take your Kleenex and get ready to laugh and cry. Enjoy the movie and tell your friends, because you will all receive a blessing.

Prayer: Father God, I praise you for the courage of the Tuohys, the movie producers, and the directors who gave you honor and glory through this portrait of Christian love. I pray that you will use this movie to advance the cause of God's kingdom and motivate Christians everywhere to reach out in the name of Christ to brothers and sisters in need. In Jesus's name, amen.

FB02:
DISCOVER YOUR STASH

1 CHRONICLES 4:9-10, MATTHEW 7:7, JOHN 10:10

Ask, and you will receive…

—Matthew 7:7

When I was a kid, the local Coca-Cola bottler sponsored a give away, placing pictures of NFL players on the inside of bottle caps. There was nothing but bottles in those days, so that meant that a lot of caps were out there. My mother taught first grade and was great friends with the principal, so I could get all the bottle caps I wanted. About twice a week, Mom would get Mrs. Bedingfield to open the drink box so that I could empty the bottle caps from the container and take them home. That container of bottle caps was like a gold mine. I spent hours sorting through the caps and pasting them to sheets that contained room for fifty or sixty different caps. I filled twenty-three sheets when I only needed five sheets for a helmet or football. When Mom and I took twenty-three sheets to the Dublin Coca-Cola bottler, the Coca-Cola employee was stunned. At first, she only wanted to give me one prize, but Mom had my back. She knew that she and I had put a lot of effort into filling up those sheets. I think I walked away with one helmet and three "official" NFL footballs.

The spiritual message of this story is that when you have special connections in life, you can get some things that you normally wouldn't get. If I had to rely on only two or three bottle caps per day, I would have never filled up those sheets. In life, we come to God with only one or two blessings in mind. He wants to give us so much more if we will only ask. I am weak in this area, and I need to push the envelope more often because I know God wants to give me the very best.

From his abundant love, God wants to give us the entire bottle cap collection of blessings. In 1 Chronicles, there is a great example of God's abundant blessing. There was a man named Jabez, who was more honorable than his brothers. Jabez offered a prayer to God, asking him to "bless me indeed, and enlarge my territory, that your Hand would be with me, and that you would keep me from evil, that I may not cause pain!" (1 Chronicles 4:10). When Jabez added the word indeed, he asked God for blessings that would be overflowing, and he received tremendous blessings from God.

God sent Jesus to us so that we could not only enjoy life but enjoy it abundantly. But we need to live for God through love and obedience, and then we just need to ask him like Mom asked Mrs. Bedingfield for the stash of bottle caps. God wants us to ask, seek, and knock so that we can receive the riches of his blessings, including the eternal gifts of salvation, joy, peace, and love. Let God shower you with a plethora of blessings each day. When you know Christ, you become eligible for the supernatural benefits of eternal life now and forevermore.

> Prayer: Dear Father God, thank you for the bountiful abundance that you want to give me each day. Help me know that you want me to have so much more than I'm asking for. May I stay in loving obedience to you so that when I ask, I will receive. When I seek, I will find. When I knock, the door will be opened. In Jesus's name, amen.

FB03:
FIRST AND TEN

EXODUS 20:1-17, 1 JOHN 1:7

You shall have no other gods before me.

—Exodus 20:3

Hearing that your favorite team has a first and ten is a welcome relief when your team has the football. Assuming there is enough time on the clock, your team has at least three plays, maybe four, to make another first down, keep the drive alive, and go into the end zone for a touchdown. First and ten! Do it again!

Another first and ten, known as the Ten Commandments, must be first in our lives if we want to walk in the Light as he (Christ) is the Light. The Ten Commandments are paraphrased as follows: Don't have any gods before me, don't have any idols, don't take my name in vain (cursing), don't dishonor the Sabbath, don't dishonor Mom and Dad, don't steal, don't lie, don't hate (murder), don't lust (adultery and greed), and don't covet. Generation after generation in Israel could not keep the commandments. God would punish them but always preserved a remnant of his chosen people. One day, God sent Jesus to be the Savior, the longawaited Messiah of the people of Israel, and eventually, he also became the Savior of the Gentiles (non-Jews).

If you want to go to heaven, first you must repent and ask for forgiveness of the sins you have committed against God because these same Ten Commandments apply as strongly today as they did several thousand years ago. To repent means to make a 180-degree turn from your sins with the intention of never repeating them. Think about doing an about-face from your sins as you turn toward God. Remember, first and ten. First repent and ask God for forgiveness for violating the Ten, and place your trust in Christ. Otherwise, you might find yourself out of downs. Your game of life will be over, you will be lost and separated forever from the Savior of the world and our Most Holy God.

> Prayer: Most gracious and loving Father, thank you for the ten rules that teach me how I should live. May I put and keep you first in my life. In Jesus's precious name, amen.

FB04:
TRANSFORMATION
FROM THE OUTSIDE IN

JOHN 3:16, 4:7-26; ROMANS 12:2

For God so loved the world, that He gave his only begotten Son, that whosoever believes in Him, shall not perish but have everlasting life.

—John 3:16

In the fall of 1980, a new wave of UGA freshman recruits came to Athens to join an average UGA team coming off a nondescript 6–5 season. One recruit was heralded as no other Georgia recruit in history. His name was Herschel Walker. However, at a preseason practice, Coach Vince Dooley turned to an assistant and said, "I'm afraid that Herschel is just a big, stiff back." Obviously, Herschel had not shown what he could do.

He entered the first game against Tennessee in the second quarter. His first hint of stardom came when a Georgia player fumbled near the sideline. Two Tennessee defenders were poised to recover the fumble, but Herschel appeared out of nowhere and landed on the ball first. In the third quarter, Herschel exploded through two linebackers and proceeded to run directly over Bill Bates for a touchdown. Bates would play thirteen years in the

NFL. UGA won 16–15, and the team knew when number 34 Walker was in the lineup, they had a chance to beat anybody.

Herschel transformed the Bulldogs into national contenders and led the team to a perfect 12–0 season and a national championship. There hasn't been one like him at Georgia before or after, but someday there will be a back that will eclipse Herschel's records. By the way, Herschel accomplished all of these feats as a child of God, a born-again Christian.

There hasn't been one like Jesus Christ. Jesus also came from the outside because he was from outside the world, not of this world. Jesus was not a product of this world. Jesus Christ came into the world as the Messiah, though he certainly didn't look like the Messiah that the Jews expected. The Jews expected a powerful ruler on a white horse, not a helpless baby. (Note: That version is coming later.) But Jesus provided the world with the Transformation with a capital *T* that it so desperately needed.

Jesus can bring you that same transformation, but first he must come from the outside into your life. Jesus first brought transformation for the woman at the well by helping her see the reasons that she was a sinner, which convinced her of her need for God's grace. She received forgiveness from Jesus and couldn't quit telling others about the living water that Jesus gave her. The only way that Jesus can come inside is by allowing his precious blood that washed on the cross to cover your sins when you repent. Repentance simply means turning from sin and wanting nothing to do with it any longer. You can't be saved by repentance, but you can't be saved without it. Once you repent and invite Christ into your life, God sends a person, the Holy Spirit, to live inside you. You will still sin because no one is perfect, but you will no longer be held in condemnation for your sin. Ask God for forgiveness and a fresh transformation daily through prayer and his holy Word to keep you in tune with his perfect plan for your life.

Prayer: Dear heavenly Father, I am so grateful that Jesus came from the outside into my heart to transform me. Now that Jesus is in my heart and the Holy Spirit lives in me, help me be transformed daily through the power of prayer and the Bible. In Jesus's name, amen.

FB05:
CLING TO THE ROCK

PSALM 62:6-7, MATTHEW 7:24-27

I will liken him to a wise man, who built his house on the rock.

—Matthew 7:24

The University of Georgia won the National Championship in 1980 behind the heroic performances of sensational freshman running back Herschel Walker. I still tease Becca that I married her for good luck after the 1980 season, because she went to every game with me, and UGA went 12–0. But the 1981 season would kick off at Clemson's Death Valley. There was a tremendous amount of excitement because Clemson had its best team ever, and tickets were very difficult to find. Becca and I searched outside the stadium for almost two hours and managed to find two in Section GG just before kickoff. On the way to the stadium, I asked a fan where Section GG was. He laughed and said, "Oh, that's green grass. You're on the hill that the Clemson team runs down." Becca and I managed to squeeze our way to the top of the hill with the Clemson behemoths just a few feet from us.

That's when I spied the Death Valley Rock. Frank Howard, the legendary coach of the Tigers for many years, placed a rock from Death Valley, California, in Clemson's Death Valley to create an intimidating aura for opposing teams. The monument for the rock was concrete and about four feet square. I cleverly told Becca that we could sit with our backs against the monument and watch the game. When the team ran down the hill, I patiently waited until the last player came by me. But nobody else did. The Clemson students swarmed the hill to get good seats behind the goalpost. I was bumped and lost my balance. I realized that Becca was being swept away from me and was in danger of being trampled. Reflexively, I reached and grabbed the rock with my left hand, and I wrapped my right arm around her waist. Becca was really upset, and we never did sit against the monument. In fact, we didn't even sit on the hill. We wandered around for a quarter and finally squeezed into the other end zone. The Dawgs turned it over nine times and lost the number one ranking to the eventual national champions, the Clemson Tigers. What a day to forget.

But don't forget this important fact from the book of Matthew. When life sweeps you off your feet and you're about to tumble down the hill, take one step, reach out as far as you can, and cling to God, the Rock of Ages. Psalm 62 proclaims that God alone is our rock, our salvation, and our refuge. Therefore, you should not be fearful when trouble comes. Don't wait until you're in trouble to reach for his help.

> Prayer: Most gracious and merciful Father, thank you for always being there for me whenever I am in danger and whenever I need a friend. Thanks for holding on to me so I don't tumble down the hill. In Jesus's name, amen.

FB06:
WHO NEEDS THE O-LINE? WE'VE GOT THE A-LINE!

LUKE 15:10, ROMANS 8:28, REVELATION 5:11

I heard the voices of many angels round about the throne…

—Revelation 5:11 (KJV)

One of the most important aspects of a football team is the offensive line, or the O-line. When the O-line opens huge holes for the powerful, swift running backs, this group of unsung heroes makes it possible to move the ball down the field. The O-line performs another important duty when the members work together to perform a protective pocket around the quarterback when he drops back to pass. This pocket of protection keeps the quarterback from being tackled before he passes the ball to his swift set of receivers. Only during replays is it obvious that the O-line made it possible for the QB, the running backs, and the receivers to shine. Without an effective O-line, a team stands little chance to win.

Just as the O-line protects the quarterback from injury, God uses his legions of angels to keep us safe. Perhaps there have been times when you have faced grave danger but somehow you came through unscathed. When we get to heaven, I believe that we will understand just how many times the angels' line of defense, the A-line, came through for us. God likely used angels to protect Daniel in the lion's den and to protect David as the young lad slew Goliath. God used an angel, whom some believe was Jesus, to protect Meshach, Shadrach, and Abednego in the fiery furnace. Just like the O-line, the A-line is made up of unsung heroes who don't receive nearly as much press as the Holy Trinity. Even the misunderstood Holy Spirit gets more attention. That's the way it should be, but the A-line deserves credit also. Let's take time to remember the next time we're in a close scrape and God brings us through. Maybe, just maybe, there were five angels performing a pocket of protection.

> Prayer: Dear God, help me realize that there are angels all around protecting me because you care about every detail of my life and are thinking about everything that happens around me. For that, I give you my deepest thanks. In Jesus's name, amen.

FB07:
ME AND JULIO,
DOWN BY THE SCHOOLYARD

PHILIPPIANS 3:11-14

Forgetting the past, and looking forward to what lies
ahead…

—Philippians 3:13

The 2009 Alabama–LSU football game was another classic in
that Deep South rivalry. Alabama trailed 15–10 late in the third
quarter, and touchdowns had been hard to come by for the num-
ber-two-ranked team. But Bama was third and goal on the LSU
two-yard line when star receiver Julio Jones committed a critical
error by illegally breaking the huddle. Julio had struggled in recent
games, dropping passes left and right, according to Greg, a friend
and staunch Alabama fan. Julio had not matched his preseason
All-American hype, and now this penalty. As Julio neared the
Alabama bench, Coach Nick Saban ripped off his headphones
and screamed at Julio as ninety-two thousand in Bryant-Denny
Stadium and millions more watched the CBS telecast. Bama settled for a field goal and trailed 15–13 entering the fourth quarter.
I wondered how Julio felt. Embarrassed? Probably. Humiliated?
Perhaps. Unhappy? No doubt about it for letting his team down.

Angry? That would have been me. Bama's perfect season and a trip to Atlanta for the SEC championship game hung in the balance because an LSU win could knock Alabama out of the race.

I was in Athens at Jillian's sorority parents' day dinner when I saw Julio commit the penalty. I was in the lobby, checking my bids on the silent auction. Not really. I was in the lobby watching the game on a big screen TV that was in the bar across the patio. I went back to our table and pulled out my BlackBerry to follow the score. A few minutes later, I clicked for an update and could hardly believe my eyes when I read, "TD 74 yard pass Julio Jones from Greg McElroy, Alabama 21 LSU 15." I am no Alabama fan, but I smiled and nodded. "Now that is a bounce back!" In fifteen minutes, Julio "went from the outhouse to the penthouse," as Vince Dooley once said when asked about the nature of the college coaching profession. Julio obviously did not allow his big failure to keep him from taking advantage of an opportunity to achieve a big success. He put the penalty behind him, remained focused, and made a play that helped his team achieve an important win.

The Apostle Paul gave a similar message to the people of Philippi when he said, "I am focusing all my energies on this one thing. Forgetting the past and looking forward to what lies ahead." Certainly Paul chose not to look back and dwell on his past failures when he had persecuted Christians. If you worry about the past, you will miss opportunities that God presents each day so that you can shine your light for all to see. If you sincerely confess your sinful mistakes and refuse to grovel in the land of self-pity and what could have been, God will forgive you, because Christ already paid the penalty for your sins and shortcomings. When you are sad, angry, depressed, humiliated, and embarrassed, remember that there is always hope for you as a believer through Jesus Christ. Let's learn from Julio's two plays. The next time you receive a setback that discourages you, talk to God about it. He alone can help you put that setback behind you so that you can look ahead to your next opportunity and his next blessing.

> Prayer: Dear Father God, when I get punched in the gut unfairly by life, as I struggle to get my breath back and stay true to you, may I realize that the presence of the Holy Spirit in me is there to help me overcome the setback and others that I will face. Thank you that you live in me, to guide and protect me. In Jesus's holy name, amen.

FB08:
GUT CHECK

MATTHEW 26:36-44, 27:32-50

So He left them, went away again, and prayed the third time...

—Matthew 26:44

The most successful football coaches get the maximum effort out of their defense when they need it most: at the most crucial time of the game. Exhausted, bone weary, injured, bloody, and bruised, the defensive unit must summon strength and courage to make the last stand. Fourth and goal on the one-yard line, the defensive team is leading by four, but the opponent has time for one more play. The ball is given to the star running back, who hurdles the line only to be stopped by the desperate lunge of a 215-pound linebacker, who drives the runner back only six inches short of a touchdown.

In December 2009, the top two teams, number two Alabama and number one Florida, met in the Georgia Dome, just as the top two teams, number two Alabama and number one Penn State, met in a domed stadium, the Louisiana Superdome, thirty years earlier. Alabama fans remember how linebacker Barry Krauss, number 77, drilled a Penn State runner just short of the goal line and won the National Championship for Alabama in the 1979 Sugar Bowl. Krauss hit the running back so hard that he knocked himself out. The play has been immortalized in paintings and photographs for three decades, and the goal line play was nick-named "Gut Check." I remember exactly how and where I sat in the floor when I saw the play on TV. Barry Krauss became a sideline reporter for the Alabama Football Network.

The first gut check for Jesus came in the garden of Gethsemane. Satan tried everything in his power to get Jesus to cave in so that he could score the deciding touchdown against mankind, but Jesus refused to yield to Satan. Jesus prayed to his Father in heaven on the first three downs, "Not My Will, but Thy Will be done." Jesus drank symbolically from the cup of sin that he would take to the cross that morning. Jesus struggled so might-ily to block Satan that great drops of blood came from his brow. Jesus endured a blood-soaked, savage beating at the hands of the Roman soldiers and struggled mightily to drag the cross through the streets of Jerusalem.

On fourth down, Jesus was nailed to the cross and hung for six excruciating hours. He could have called for a thousand legions of angels to take him off the cross and kick everybody's butt who had ridiculed, abused, and tortured him. Your sin and my sin nailed him to that cross, but love kept him there. On the cross, Jesus played a thousand fourth down gut checks each time he struggled to take his next breath to hang a little longer to dem-onstrate the power of his love for fallen mankind. After the skies turned black, Jesus hung for three hours, the equivalent of a foot-ball game, before he gave up the Spirit.

The next time you face a gut check and you think you can't get through it, know that Jesus already hung to make you strong. He has *been there* and *done that* just for you so that you can handle stress and strain like a saint, even discovering joy in the midst of your trials.

> Prayer: Dear Jesus, I can never repay you for your gut checks that occurred because of my sin. But I thank you with all my heart and give you my life for the ultimate price you paid for me. Thank you for your amazing love and grace, and may I live in humility and gratitude for you from this moment forward. In Jesus's name, amen.

FB09:
GOD'S PERFECT TIMING

GALATIANS 4:4, NEHEMIAH 2:5, DANIEL 9:25

> But when the fullness of time had come, God sent forth
> his Son...
>
> —Galatians 4:4

In a sports contest, timing means the difference between victory
and defeat. Consider a pass in football when the receiver runs an
out pattern by running ten yards, planting his inside foot, and
cutting sharply at 90 degrees to the sideline. The quarterback
must time the receiver's steps and deliver the football before the
receiver comes out of his break. He leads him so that the ball
arrives at the precise moment that the receiver turns to catch the
ball and drags his toes to stay in bounds. The cornerback closely
covers the receiver. If the throw is late or behind the receiver, it's
down the sidelines for a pick six (interception for a touchdown).
The timing must be perfect for the play to succeed.

God is the master of perfect timing. He sent his Son, Jesus
Christ, at the perfect time. Several positive factors were already in
play when Jesus arrived as a baby born to a virgin in a stable. The
people of Israel were frustrated by Roman rule and eager for the
Messiah that their prophets had foretold. The language of the day
in numerous countries was a Greek blend, which made it easier
for the first Christians to communicate the good news of the

gospel that Christ rose from the dead. The Roman government had built thousands of miles of roads and aqueducts that literally paved the way for the apostles and disciples of Christ to travel from country to country. Greek philosophers left the Greek people unfulfilled. All of these factors benefited the spreading of the good news.

But the reason that God's timing is perfect is because Jesus came from heaven to earth at precisely the exact time to fulfill the prophecies of the Scripture. King Artaxerxes ordered the rebuilding of the Temple walls in 445 BC. The book of Daniel predicted that the Messiah would arrive after sixty-nine "weeks." Each week actually represented a seven-year period, 69 x 7, or 483 years. Mathematicians and astronomers studied the pattern of the new moons and discovered that Jesus rode triumphantly into Jerusalem on the back of the donkey on the very day that was predicted almost five hundred years before. Our God is a mighty God. His plan for each day of your life is replete with timing. When you get in lock step with God by surrendering your life to his guidance, he has greater blessings in store for you than you could ever imagine. He will deliver those blessings in his perfect time.

> Prayer: I believe that you made the universe in six days and rested on the seventh. Help me trust that you alone know what is best for me each day, because I am your beloved child, for which I am eternally grateful. In the holy name of Jesus Christ, my Savior and Lord, amen.

FB10:
THE PREGAME SPEECH

1 CORINTHIANS 2:1-5, 9:24-25; PHILIPPIANS 3:14

And my speech and my preaching was not with enticing words of man's wisdom, but in demonstration of the Spirit and of power.

—1 Corinthians 2:4 (KJV)

There have been many great pregame speeches in the history of sports. Perhaps the most famous speech is "Win One for the Gipper." Legendary Notre Dame football coach Knute Rockne exhorted his players to win the game for their fallen teammate, George Gipp, the Gipper. On another occasion, Gale Sayers gave a very emotional speech to his Chicago Bears teammates for teammate Brian Piccolo, who would die of cancer later that season. Coach Dale, in the movie *Hoosiers*, told his basketball team that they could beat the large high school teams. He fired up his team, who came charging out of the tunnel. These talks were characterized by a person really believing passionately in their team and their cause, pleading with teammates and players to give all that they had to win the game.

The Apostle Paul pled passionately with the people of his day to win the game of life, the ultimate race and the ultimate prize. The winner receives a one-way all-expense-paid trip to heaven and gets his or her name in the official scorebook, the Book of

Life. The way to win the game of life is to surrender your heart to Christ after professing godly sorrow for your sins. God sent his Son to die for you. When you have your big game and one of God's coaches, a preacher, youth pastor, or evangelist, exhorts you to commit your life to Christ, you can come charging out of the tunnel to live for him. Are you concerned that you won't know how to play the game after you commit? Don't worry. God will take you just as you are and train you to be a Christian. As Super Bowl winning coach Tony Dungy once pointed out, God gave us his perfect Word, the Bible, to teach us how to live. He gave us prayer so that you can talk to God during the game of life anytime that you want. You can come boldly to the throne in the name of Jesus Christ to seek his guidance and listen to his advice. God gives you teammates, who are fellow believers, to help guide and transform you.

The next time you hear a pregame speech (sermon), may it be the one that transforms you and sends you charging into the game of life for Christ.

> Prayer: Father God, thank you so much for the people that you place in my life to coach me and exhort me to do greater things for your kingdom. May I have the discernment to execute on their godly instructions and wisdom. In Jesus's name, amen.

FB11:
TWO-MINUTE DRILL

1 CORINTHIANS 9:22, 2 CORINTHIANS 5:17, JAMES 4:14-15

For what is your life? It is even a vapor that appears for a little time, and then vanishes away.

—James 4:14

A football team that trails late in the fourth quarter employs the two-minute drill. Made famous by Baltimore Colts quarterback Johnny Unitas in the 1958 NFL Championship game, this offensive tactic is designed to move the ball quickly downfield with a series of quick passes. After each play, the offense hurries to the line of scrimmage to save precious time on the clock. One more pass is completed, and the clock ticks six, five, four, three seconds. The quarterback takes the snap, spikes the ball into the turf, and trudges wearily off the field as the field goal kicker comes in to try to save the game with a last-second miracle kick. But why did the team wind up in such a desperate predicament? Perhaps it was because of a series of fumbles, interceptions, penalties, and missed opportunities in the first fifty-eight minutes of the game. This accumulation of errors made it necessary to deploy the hurry-up offense to atone for squandered chances.

How does your walk with Christ look today? Have you lost precious time on the clock to serve him? Do you need a last-second miracle to save you? Perhaps you say, "Oh, I'm (your age). I have (seventy minus your age) years to get right with Jesus. Until then, I'll have my fun." That is a risky position to take. God gives you today. His mercies are new every morning. Jesus took the final spike two thousand years ago so that you could be free of all of the mistakes, the botched personal relationships, bad business deals, selfish decisions, and all the times you've put yourself ahead of him and your loved ones.

Here is a two-minute drill that can save your life right now, right where you're sitting, for eternity. Stop and reflect for a moment. Why is this not the perfect time to shed my old life for a new life in Christ? You don't have to be in church to come to Christ. You don't need to accomplish one more thing in your life or perform another good deed. God will take you right where you are, no matter how old or young you are. You just need to tell God in your own words how truly sorry you are that you have lived a sinful life. Then tell him that you want a new life in Christ, whom you believe died on the cross for your sins, and he will give you that fresh start.

I invite you to pray this prayer, and it's the attitude of your heart that matters most.

> Prayer: Lord Jesus, I realize that I can't do it my way any longer. I have sinned against you and God, and I need you to cleanse me now with the blood that you shed on the cross for me. You paid my penalty so that I don't get penalized for eternity. Please come into my new heart and give me a new life. Take control and start making me the person you want me to be. Thank you for making me a child of God and for the free gift of grace that I do not deserve but readily accept. You made my new life possible when you died on the cross and rose from the grave. In Jesus's holy and precious name, amen.

Two minutes. That's all it took to change your life for eternity. If you believe that you sincerely took off the old self and put on the new self, go tell somebody right now so that you can receive support and prayer.

> Prayer: Father God, how marvelous is your grace that it costs me only two minutes to get right with you forever. But it cost Jesus his life and searing pain and agony, and I thank you for sending Jesus to die for me. Thank you, Jesus, for paying the penalty for me. In Jesus's name, amen.

FB12:
GOD'S PLAYBOOK

PSALM 12:6-7, 2 TIMOTHY 3:16

The words of the Lord are pure words: as silver tried in a
furnace of earth, purified seven times.

—Psalm 12:6

One of the teenagers in Sunday school class boldly proclaimed
that the Bible has many contradictions, particularly in the book
of Leviticus. At the time, I didn't explain well why the Bible is
indeed the perfect Word of God that was inspired by God. I did
say that there are a lot of things that I don't understand, but I
accept what is in the Bible by faith.

Afterward, I thought of a sports analogy. Let's suppose that
the playbook of a football team contains two hundred different
plays. Suppose one player decided that he didn't like play number
fourteen and ripped it out of the playbook. The offensive coordinator calls for play number fourteen on the last play of the
ball game even though it hadn't been used all season. Guess who
didn't know where to line up? It cost the team a delay-of-game
penalty, and the player was benched for the next game. Suppose
a lineman chose to change the blocking scheme for a pass play.
He doesn't pick up the blitzing linebacker, who blindsides his
quarterback. The quarterback winds up with a concussion and is

out for the season. Obviously, you cannot have players changing or deleting plays in the playbook or chaos will reign.

So why do people change the Bible to suit their needs? By ignoring certain books of the Old Testament, essentially tearing plays out of God's playbook, you will never understand how the New Testament meshes perfectly with the prophecies of the Old Testament. When you consciously apply your interpretation, you put yourself above God.

The Way of the Master Bible, by evangelist Ray Comfort, provides excellent guidance in helping Christians tackle many challenging and difficult interpretations of the Bible. I realize that God's ways are above my ways. To the best of my ability, I believe that God's playbook, the Bible, is inspired by God, spoken by him through more than forty authors of sixty-six books that came together seamlessly over a fifteen-hundred-year period. Either you believe the Bible is the truth, the whole truth, and nothing but the truth, or it's a complete lie. Friends, there is no middle ground.

When Billy Graham was a young preacher, he had doubts about portions of the Bible. But one moonlit night, Billy got on his knees in a field and told God that he didn't understand it all but from that point forward, he would believe it all. No more changing plays or ripping plays out of the playbook for young Billy. It's no wonder at all that soon, his preaching and career as an evangelist took off.

Do you believe all the plays in God's playbook? That decision will have a major impact on God's ability to use you as a major player in his offense to advance his kingdom. God's playbook is our guide for Christian discipleship. There is a reason that the Bible has withstood the test of time. When this world ends, two things will live in the new heaven. Those two things are believers and the living Word of God. God spoke the Word into being, and the Word later became flesh in Christ (John 1:14). Since

Jesus was and is perfect, then the living Word of God is perfect. The case is closed.

> Prayer: Father God, thank you for your perfect Living Word. May I yearn for the knowledge that is obtained through the study of your precepts. You have given us your perfect playbook that each person can follow for wisdom, discernment, and living a life that brings glory and honor to you. In Jesus's name, amen.

FB13:
NONE GO UNDEFEATED
(SAVE ONE)

ISAIAH 45:5, 22; ROMANS 3:23, 1 JOHN 5:21

I am the Lord, and there is no other. There is no God besides Me.

—Isaiah 45:5

The 2009 college football regular season ended with a modern-day record: five unbeaten teams. The fan bases were all fired up, and when each team eventually lost again, it's a sure thing that some fans screamed, "Why did you call that pass play on third and goal?" Oklahoma won forty-seven in a row in the 1950s, but when OU finally lost 7–0 in Norman, the OU fans sat in stunned silence that their team could possibly lose a game.

No team stays undefeated. No person stays unblemished. When you make someone an idol, it is inevitable that the person will eventually let you down. No matter how hard Israel tried to keep the Ten Commandments with their 613 laws, nobody could do it, not even Saul of Tarsus.

The higher you put somebody on a pedestal and the more you live your life through a person, the greater the shock when that person falls short physically, morally, or spiritually. It's very dangerous to worship idols because you set yourself up for heartache and disappointment.

I remember vividly when I was twenty-two years old when my idol, Pete Maravich, blew out his knee at the zenith of his career. The Atlanta Hawks traded Pete to the expansion New Orleans Jazz, and the Jazz had never made the playoffs. But the Jazz rode an eight-game winning streak, and the city was abuzz with play-off fever. With a few minutes to play and the Jazz up by twenty over Buffalo, Pete entertained the Superdome crowd by whipping a between-the-legs pass down court to a teammate for a slam dunk. But the courtside patrons heard a sickening pop. Pete grabbed his right knee and writhed in pain.

I was listening to the game on a scratchy AM radio as I often did. I had pulled for Pete to have success because he was tagged a loser by some, even though he was the franchise player. In just four days, Pete would have returned to Atlanta for the NBA All-Star Game as basketball's best player at the time. Pete would show the Hawks how wrong they were to trade him, coming back to star in my city, and I would be at the game to see it all. It just was not fair. I went to the game, but I had a strange, detached feeling.

That type of reaction occurs when your goals that are totally outside your control are not realized. The reaction happens when you god up an idol and put the idol above God, breaking the first two of the Ten Commandments. I didn't know Jesus Christ when I was twenty-two. But that's where knowing Christ would have given me a huge advantage. As a believer, you remember that Jesus is number one after the disappointment and realize that no matter who or what disappointed you, your future is secure in heaven thanks to the One who took your place.

Pete never reached the same level of play after the injury and bitterly quit basketball several years later after never achieving his goal of playing for a world championship. But he found joy and peace in Jesus Christ after his playing days. Today, Pete Maravich's name is still in many record books, and it's in the only record book that matters: the Book of Life. And so is mine. How about yours? God planned before you were born for your name to be there too.

> Prayer: Father God, may I maintain perspective when I am disappointed by my team and my favorite athlete or when someone I love hurts me. May I remember the eternal game that I won when I repented and accepted Christ, and may I forgive as you forgave me for my sins through Jesus's death on the cross. In Jesus's holy name, amen.

FB14:
TIM TEBOW

PHILIPPIANS 1:6

Being confident of this very thing, that He who has begun a good work in you will complete it until the day of Jesus Christ.

Tim Tebow became the first-ever college sophomore to win the famed Heisman trophy in the seventy-three-year history of the award. He played four years at the University of Florida and received All-American honors. Tebow currently plays quarterback for the Denver Broncos of the NFL. Upon receiving the 2007 Heisman Trophy, Tim offered these reflections on the priority in his life of football and the award.

"I'd just like to first start off by thanking my Lord and Savior, Jesus Christ, who gave me the ability to play football and gave me a great family and a support group and great coaches and everything around me," a breathless Tebow said at the ceremony, moments after the award was announced.

Football rates a mere fourth on his list of priorities behind God, family, and academics. In a profile aired on ESPN during the Heisman award ceremony, Tebow said that his priorities are, "Number one, my faith in God; number two, my family and my relationships with my family; number three, academics; and number four is football."

Prayer: Dear Father, it is so refreshing when a famous athlete has the proper perspective of priorities in his life. May Tim continue to reach many people throughout his career for the kingdom of God. In Jesus's holy name, amen.

FB15:
RUN, FORREST!

GENESIS 39:7-21, MATTHEW 5:23-28, 1 CORINTHIANS 6:18-20

Run from sexual sin!

—1 Corinthians 6:18 (NLT)

One of the most memorable movies of the past few decades was *Forrest Gump*. Tom Hanks played the role of a young man from Greenbow, Alabama, who suffered from a mild form of autism. Yet everything he did turned to gold, from buying a shrimp boat in Bayou Le Batre, to saving the life of Lieutenant Dan in Vietnam, to becoming a professional table tennis player after rehabbing from being shot in the "butt-ocks."

The movie opens with Forrest as a young boy being teased mercilessly by the neighborhood boys for being slow-witted and having braces on both legs. As his young friend Jenny screams, "Run, Forrest!" Forrest runs frantically to escape them. His leg braces literally disintegrate and fly from his legs as he pulls away from the boys. His next running escapade occurs when he plays football for the University of Alabama. Forrest fields a kickoff and runs toward the sideline as the coaches and players frantically direct him to run toward the goal line. He scores and runs through the end zone and out of the stadium. When his beloved

Jenny leaves him after reconnecting as adults, Forrest runs to forget her. He runs across the United States and starts the jogging craze.

There is one place in the Bible that says we are to run from sin. Paul exhorted the people of Corinth who were accustomed to immoral sexual practices to "Run from sexual sin!" These people were sinning, and Paul yelled at them to run from their evil ways. Paul shouted at them like the Alabama players, coaches, fans, and the way his dear mother and his Jenny did: "Run, Forrest!" That picture is a good one to keep in your mind when your eyes linger for a second look and your mind starts to wander. Avoid that second look, turn away, and run.

Potiphar's wife tried to seduce Joseph. When she grabbed his garment and begged him to be with her, he fled. Although Joseph was wrongly accused and placed in prison, he also was shown great mercy by God and became the second most powerful man in Egypt. When you run from sexual sin, it might not seem like much, but God will reward you for that small victory. God has a special mate picked out for you, and the more you entrust your thoughts to honorable ways when temptation arises, the more special that relationship will become for you. If you continuously cave into sexual temptations, you will distort your view of the opposite sex, damage your future relationship, or miss it altogether.

There was one time in the movie that Forrest should have run, but he didn't. Jenny walked into Forrest's bedroom one evening and seduced him. She later gave birth to his son. Having sex outside of marriage is a sin according to the Bible. Most Hollywood filmmakers and TV producers create storylines that would lead you to believe that there are no negative consequences from premarital sex. Making a vow to abstain from sex until marriage may seem weak in the eyes of the world, but in God's eyes it is very honorable and demonstrates obedience to him.

Keep yourself pure and honorable by running from sexual sin, and God will honor you with blessings that are much better than cheap thrills.

> Prayer: Father God, never has there been a time with more temptations to commit lustful sins. Keep me strong in my daily decisions to run from sexual sin and run to you and your Word. I believe that you will honor those right decisions one day through my future relationship with the person who is just right for me. In Jesus's holy and precious name, amen.

FB16:
CHRISTMAS IN ALABAMA

2 CORINTHIANS 4:18, ROMANS 8:18,
1 THESSALONIANS 4:13-17, REVELATION 21:1-5

We look not at what can be seen, but what cannot be seen.
For what can be seen is temporary, but what cannot be
seen is eternal.

—2 Corinthians 4:18 (TLB)

When I was a kid in Middle Georgia, on Christmas Day, my family would have Santa Claus and our Christmas tree, pack our suitcases, and be on the road to northwest Alabama by nine o'clock. Each Christmas Day, my mother would meet her brothers and sisters at my grandmother's house in Hamilton, Alabama, which was 387 miles of lonely, two-lane roads away. I decided back then that I would never travel with my family on Christmas Day.

One Christmas Day, we couldn't find a restaurant open to get a hamburger. Dad pulled up to a greasy spoon around two in the afternoon. He decided not to go inside because they served beer. That was admirable and made a lasting impression on me, but I was still hungry. When I was eight, Santa brought me a full football uniform with shoulder pads and padded football pants and new cowboy boots. I wanted so badly to go out in my yard and play with my football and feel the ground as my pads collided with the grass, but there wasn't time. We had to go to Alabama. We needed to leave then or we would be late for supper. Who cares? Guess what I wore for the next 387 miles? Finally, we pulled up the gravel driveway at my grandmother's house. I leaped out of the car and begged my brother to throw me a pass after nine hours of anticipation.

Do I look forward to the celebration of the birth of Jesus with the same anticipation and excitement? Do I have that same type of longing for the Second Coming of our Savior and Lord? Look around us at the pain, suffering, and humiliation that this world brings. The book of Revelation assures us that there will be no more sorrow and no more pain forever. The Bible assures us that complete joy will be ours one day when we know Christ and he knows us. But we will not look forward daily to his coming or our departure if we allow the temporary trappings of this world to dominate our thoughts.

When is the last time you thought of eternity? If you are not a believer, eternity is the last thing that you think about because you don't want to face the truth. If you are a believer, you should look forward eagerly with anticipation to the new heaven and the new earth when Jesus comes to reign supreme, sort of like I did when I eagerly caught my first pass after waiting all day. I hope that you wait eagerly to see Jesus face to face.

> Prayer: Father God, thank you for the memories of the special Christmas presents that stay fondly with me through the years. Most of all, thank you for the birth of your Son who came to save me. Help me live in a way that I eagerly wait for my face-to-face meeting with Jesus, either in heaven or in the clouds, should he come back first. In Jesus's name, amen.

FB17:
HEISMAN HYPE

JOSHUA 1:8, MATTHEW 7:7, PHILIPPIANS 4:19, 2 CORINTHIANS 4:18

> But my God shall supply all your need according to His riches in glory by Christ Jesus.
>
> —Philippians 4:19 (KJV)

For the past seventy years, the New York City Downtown Athletic Club has awarded the Heisman trophy to the player who is selected as the top collegiate football player in America. Note that I did not say the best player, because the best player in the country is more likely to achieve success in the NFL than the typical Heisman winner. Winning the Heisman trophy has never guaranteed the same level of success in the NFL. Heisman winners Doug Flutie and Johnny Rodgers actually began their careers in the inferior Canadian Football League. Still others had mediocre careers in the NFL. Rarely does the Heisman winner turn out to be the MVP in the NFL.

The Bible teaches us that there is no guarantee of success without God and Jesus Christ at the center of our lives. Joshua 1:8 instructs us to do according to all that is written in the Bible. How will we ever know to do all that is written in it unless we *know* all that is written in it? Don't be discouraged if you know very little of the Bible in the beginning. The main point is to read or meditate on Scripture each day, and it might be for only a few minutes.

If we love God and are obedient to God by trying to do all that is written in the Bible, we will receive prosperity. It will not be prosperity as the world measures it (fame, money, awards, plaques, and trophies) but as God measures it, through our willingness to share his love with our fellow man. For then we will not only find prosperity and riches, but we will know success as God measures success. Our achievement of success as believers will one day manifest itself in a special crown that awaits us in heaven.

Satan hypes stuff that we can see and touch as the key to happiness, but that hype is untrue. The college football Heisman winner is hyped as the greatest player, but he has no guarantee of success in the NFL. As a believer, you are guaranteed success as a disciple of Christ at your next level, which is the eternal level because the Holy Spirit lives within you. Once you receive Christ, you are eternal and will live forever with him.

God promises you untold riches in accordance with his plan for your life and through his mercy and grace. If you discover where God is working, he will use you to achieve victories for his kingdom. No Heisman winner will ever have anything on you.

Prayer: Dear most gracious and loving Father, help me discover the real riches that you have planned for me, not the earthly trappings that men gloat over but the internal riches of peace, joy, and love. Only through you and your Son can I ever achieve the good tidings of success and prosperity that come through a personal relationship with the Trinity. In Jesus's name, amen.

FB18:
THE POSTGAME PRESS
CONFERENCE

PSALM 7:11-13, ROMANS 2:1-16, 2 PETER 2:9

The Lord knows how to deliver the godly out of temptations, and to reserve the unjust to the day of judgment to
be punished.

—2 Peter 2:9

Imagine that you are the head coach of a major college football
team with a fervent fan base. Your team just suffered its fifth consecutive loss to your bitter in-state rival. Your team committed
four turnovers and performed with a lackluster effort in the second half as you got your doors blown off 48–17 at home, and your
fans left in droves in the middle of the third quarter. Now it's
time to face the music of the postgame press conference. As you
trudge toward the press conference room, you recall that tomorrow night, you get to spend a whole hour with some of the most
frustrated fans in the country on your statewide call-in show.

Who among us could stand up to the heat that comes from
press conferences, call-in shows, blogs, and chat boards? How did
you lose control of your team? When are you going to fire your
offensive coordinator? Why did your players quit in the fourth

quarter? Rumors swirl around the state that you will be fired by sundown tomorrow. What would be your reaction to all of these rumors? About 99.9 percent of us would be completely overwhelmed if we were suddenly thrust into a situation for which we are totally unprepared.

You had better believe that the coach's postgame press conference is a tough situation in those circumstances. But one day you could find yourself in a situation that is much tougher and infinitely more important and fearful. That's when you take the stand at the day of judgment. Each man and woman passes from this earth and comes before God one on one at the throne of our most holy God. Unless Jesus turns to the Questioner and says, "I will take all of your questions." That is the beauty of judgment day when you are a believer. Jesus will handle judgment day with God for you, and you will never have to face God. That alone is worth coming to Christ, isn't it?

If you are not a believer, one who has earnestly turned from sin and accepted Christ as your Savior, then you are in for one tough press conference. How could a person ever justify and explain to God about the times that he or she has been unfaithful and wasted time chasing the trappings and lures of the world? What a relief it is to know that Jesus will speak on our behalf at the pearly gates instead of silence before the abyss. This type of postgame press conference is inevitable. Prepare now.

> Prayer: Father God, thank you for the perfect goodness of your mercy and grace that Jesus can represent me, a sinner washed in the blood of the Lamb. I pray to you now that (my friend) who will face you at judgment will come to know Jesus as Savior and Lord. In Jesus's name, amen.

FB19:
PRACTICE MAKES PERFECT

PHILIPPIANS 1:6

Being confident of this very thing, that He who has begun a good work in you will complete it until the day of Jesus Christ.

When I was a kid in Middle Georgia, I was a big Green Bay Packers fan. I loved the green-and-gold uniforms with the oval G on the helmet. I knew the names and numbers of every starter and most of the substitutes. My friend from Wisconsin stared at me like I was from another planet when, as an adult, I rattled off the mid-1960s starting offensive line, "Skoronski 76, Thurston 63, Ringo 50, Kramer 64, and Gregg 75."

The Packers won five NFL championships in the sixties, including the first two Super Bowls, under legendary coach Vince Lombardi. Coach Lombardi was a disciplinarian and drilled into his players the need to execute plays perfectly. One play the Packers perfected was the Green Bay power sweep. The Packers would pull the right guard on running plays around left end and vice versa. This maneuver outnumbered the defenders and opened huge holes for halfback Paul Hornung and fullback Jim Taylor. No matter how the defense prepared, the Packers seemed to get the first down and touchdown they needed when they ran this play.

Training camp would open in July under miserably hot conditions. Even though the veterans knew this play like the backs of their hands, Lombardi would have them run it again and again and again. Some players probably ran the play thousands of times over the course of their careers. Lombardi didn't just run it in July and never practiced it again because he knew that in December, the timing would be off and the play would break down at the most crucial time. He would no longer have his go-to play, his bread-and-butter play, without that repetitious practice.

Your life as a Christian resembles the Green Bay power sweep. You become a Christian when you get it for the first time and become converted. But the schemes that Satan throws against you each day are powerful and designed to knock you off track. That's why the discipline of daily prayer and reading the Bible and study becomes important. Sure, you know the story of the gospel by heart, and the birth of Jesus and his death and resurrection, but your timing is thrown off little by little if you don't practice daily. One day when you need it most, you find that you've lost your power because you allowed the world to rule you instead of God's plan. God even gives you an extra blocker, the Holy Spirit, to overcome Satan and rip huge holes in his defense. Your dedication and renewal each day allows you to open holes for others to become believers through your words, deeds, and actions in the name of Christ. Satan knows it's coming, but he can't stop it. Satan's strength is always weaker than God's strength. You have the supernatural strength of God when you practice daily blocking and tackling through prayer and Bible study.

> Prayer: Thank you, Father God, for the power sweep O-line of God, Jesus, the Holy Spirit, prayer, and Bible study that enables me to avoid the obstacles that Satan presents. I praise you for sending me Jesus to save me from myself. In Jesus's name, amen.

FB20: CAMPFIRE, BONFIRE, OR FOREST FIRE?

1 CORINTHIANS 3:9-15, REVELATION 1:8-13, COLOSSIANS 3:17

> But if the house he has built burns up, he will suffer a great loss. He himself will be saved, but like a man escaping through a wall of flames.
>
> —1 Corinthians 3:15 (TLB)

One of the great traditions in high school and college sports is homecoming week. A big event at many homecoming celebrations on the eve of the big game is the bonfire. On Thursday and Friday fall nights on campuses across America, students, faculty, and friends thrill at the sight of a blazing bonfire as faces are warmed and friendship bonds are strengthened. Fans eagerly anticipate the exciting game the following day.

Perhaps the greatest bonfire tradition was at Texas A&M University in College Station, Texas. A team of cadets would be assigned each year to construct the bonfire, and the competition to build the tallest bonfire ever was intense. One year, the stack of wood reached over one hundred feet into the sky. Unfortunately, a tragic accident occurred that resulted in the loss of precious lives, and the bonfire celebration was postponed. A wonderful tradition had unfortunately become a shocking, horrendous tragedy.

The book of Revelation promises that Jesus will look upon the words, deeds, and actions that you and I accumulate over a lifetime. Jesus will look upon our events that are stacked like cordwood. Those deeds that were performed in the name of Jesus will be purified like silver refined seven times and burnished gold and will last for eternity. Those actions that were performed for selfish reasons and personal glory will be incinerated. Poof!

Think about the life that you've lived thus far and how you spend your spare time. Maybe there is a reason you don't have spare time. Are you working for God or mostly working for yourself? If you've consistently worked for God to achieve victories for his kingdom, your fire will more closely resemble a campfire. The more selfish the acts, the greater the fire. Would your accomplishments turn into burnished gold or a huge bonfire or a raging forest fire? Determine from this day forward that your private time will include plenty of acts to advance God's kingdom and that you include God in your work or school. If your words and deeds include God, then they won't go up in smoke.

> Prayer: Father God, thank you for the knowledge in your Word that my selfish deeds will one day go up in smoke. May I use this knowledge when I'm sitting around and have a choice to do something for me or do something for God. In Jesus's name, amen.

FB21:
ALL-ACCESS PASS

MATTHEW 27:51, HEBREWS 4:16

And behold, the veil of the temple was torn in two from the top to the bottom...

—Matthew 27:51

If you've ever been to a large sporting event, you'll notice that there is a pecking order. There is a big difference between the nosebleed and courtside seats. There is nothing like an all-access pass that allows you to go anywhere in the arena or stadium. An all-access pass at the Masters Golf Tournament is equivalent to getting into the press room, the clubhouse, and out on the veranda near the putting green. It's cool to even be at Augusta, but eventually, you find yourself staring at the people on the clubhouse grounds at the tables under the giant oak tree. You wonder what it would be like to be on the other side of the ropes. At the 2010 BCS Championship game, an all-access pass got you onto the field before and after the game. My daughter Allison's boyfriend, Kevin, got a sideline pass to the Alabama–Texas game, and she wished that she could have been there with him. At the NBA Finals, you could stand in the tunnel next to Kobe or Lebron just before they jog onto the floor. Anybody who has been to the Final Four would love to be courtside to see the interaction between players, coaches, and officials in the high-pressure game situation.

An all-access pass at a concert would get you onto the back of the stage as performers excite the crowd with well-known songs.

In the Old Testament days, the only person with an all-access pass was the chief priest. But the chief priest could only go behind the veil in the holy of holies once a year, sort of like Super Bowl Sunday comes once a year. On that day, the chief priest cleansed himself before entering the holy of holies and presenting the sacrifices before God. That was the one day a year that someone interacted with God.

But Jesus changed all of that. After God could no longer look upon the sins that his Son carried to the cross, the temple walls collapsed and that curtain was torn in two forever. The tearing of the curtain indicated that all people now had 24/7 access to God through Jesus Christ, who sits as our intercessor when we talk with God. Jesus is the all-access pass that everyone needs to come boldly to God's throne.

> Prayer: God, how awesome it is that I can come to you at any time, night or day, when I need to talk. Help me remember that there are many times that you want to come talk with me. In Jesus's name, amen.

FB22:
KNOCKING ON THE DOOR

REVELATION 3:20, 2 CORINTHIANS 5:17, TITUS 3:5

Behold, I stand at the door and knock.

—Revelation 3:20

The University of Georgia football team had a legendary announcer named Larry Munson for over forty years. Larry was best known for his dramatic, emotional calls of famous plays in Georgia history. When UGA drove down the field and got inside the opponent's twenty-yard line, Munson would shout, "Georgia's knocking on the door! They're on the Tennessee sixteen!" That line reminds me of Revelation 3:20: "Behold, I stand at the door and knock. If anyone hears my voice and opens the door, I will come into him and dine with him and him with me."

Do you realize that until you become a believer, Jesus waits patiently at the door of your heart every day, knocking politely, waiting for you to invite him in? The next time you see your front door, imagine that Jesus is sitting on the doorstep, waiting to be invited into your home. However, there is no doorknob to the door of your heart on the outside. There is only a doorknob on the inside of your heart, and only you can turn it to open the door of your heart for Christ. Jesus will never force his way into your heart. If Jesus did, it wouldn't be your decision, would it? And

God has given each person free will to decide how to live his or her life. Only when you say in your heart, *I am sick and tired of this sinful, hypocritical life that I'm living, and I want to shed the old me for a new me!* will Jesus come through the door and into your life for eternity. You can repent, open the door, and make him your Savior today. Come, Lord Jesus.

> Prayer: Lord Jesus, thank you for waiting patiently for me each day. Father God, thank you for the second, third, fourth, and hundredth chance that you have given me. You are so loving, kind, and merciful. In Jesus's name, amen.

FB23:
WILL YOU ACKNOWLEDGE THE
CLAMOR OF THE COWBELLS?

JEREMIAH 1:5-6, EZEKIEL 36:26,
MATTHEW 3:1, 4:17

Before you came forth out of the womb, I sanctified you,
and I ordained you a prophet of the nations.

—Jeremiah 1:5

Becca and I traveled to Tupelo, Mississippi, to spend the night
with our friends, Frank and Ginger. The next morning, we all
headed to Starkville for the Georgia–Mississippi State game.
Herschel Walker was a junior, and when Herschel played, Becca
and I didn't miss a game, home or away. We were confident
that UGA would win, but Starkville presented a unique challenge called cowbells. Thousands of Mississippi State fans owned
cowbells that were painted maroon and white and adorned with
fraternity logos and other decorations. Together, these cowbells
made a horrendous clatter. Before the game, I heard the fans rat-
tle the cowbells. I turned to my friend, Frank, and said, "Frank,
I thought the SEC outlawed the use of cowbells inside the stadium. Look at those people. How did they get those cowbells in
the stadium?"

Frank looked at me with a straight face and said with all sincerity, "Cowbells? I don't hear any cowbells." He turned to his friend Bruce and asked, "Bruce, do you hear any cowbells?"

Bruce shook his head. "Frank, I don't hear any cowbells either."

Obviously, they were both pulling my leg. UGA won the game despite the clamor of cowbells throughout the game.

Frank's remark about not hearing any cowbells is how some people react to hearing the gospel. Frank didn't acknowledge the cowbells even though he heard them because he enjoyed the advantage the noise gave Mississippi State. I sat in church for years and heard the gospel preached. I heard the preacher, but I didn't hear the gospel because I never internalized the message due to a hardened heart that kept me from hearing the message clearly. Our Methodist ministers preached a comfortable gospel that rarely mentioned sin and certainly never mentioned hell. If I wasn't hearing sin on Sunday, and I certainly wasn't reading about sin during the week, being Bible ignorant, I continued to dwell in the bliss of my ignorance.

God has sent noisemakers to clang the cowbells for thousands of years in the form of prophets, preachers, and evangelists. From John the Baptist to Isaiah to Jeremiah to Ezekiel to Daniel to Hosea, the prophets rang the cowbells, warning of the judgment to come, but so often, the message fell on the deaf ears of the Israeli people. Sadly, many people today will hear the gospel but choose not to follow Jesus because of comfortable living and hardened hearts. Praise God that I finally heard when my favorite athlete explained how he heard the good news of Jesus Christ.

If you don't know Christ, the likelihood that you will respond to the gospel decreases as you get older. You get a little deafer because your hardened heart makes the gospel bounce away. You achieve an impressive track record of worldly success but give God none of the credit. You're afraid that your good life will change if you give into living like the preacher. But your good life will eventually lead to ruin and destruction. Isn't it time that you acknowledged the clatter of the gospel cowbells and turned to Christ?

> Prayer: Father God, thank you for sending the prophets of yesteryear and today to share the good news of the gospel. I pray for a new enlightenment among my friends who need Christ but refuse to hear the clang of the warning. I thank you daily for the mercy and grace you showed me and show me still. In Jesus's name, amen.

FB24:
ARE YOU DEPENDING ON A LAST-SECOND MIRACLE?

JOHN 6:44, MATTHEW 6:30, ACTS 5:1-5

The Father will draw you to the Son…

—John 6:44 (paraphrased)

Each fall weekend, several college or pro games are decided by a last-second field goal attempt. Either the field goal is good and the offense wins or the field goal is missed and the defense wins. The field goal kicker, the specialist of all football players, warms up his leg on the sideline and is suddenly thrust front and center under a white-hot spotlight as the opposing fans scream for the kicker to miss a kick that is usually between thirty and fifty yards. The kicker must send the ball between two posts that look no wider than a car from that distance. The game, possibly a title, hangs in the balance. The snapper must deliver the ball crisply to the holder. Every lineman must block well and not jump offside. The holder must catch the ball, place it on the spot, and twirl the ball to place the laces away from the kicker. The kicker must plant his foot securely and deliver a perfectly timed kick. The ball must be kicked high, far, and accurately. If the opponent doesn't block it, then the kicker's team might just win the game. Pretty simple? Hardly.

Naturally, any number of plays better executed during the game could have prevented this last-gasp effort. Will your opportunity to know Christ and receive God's free gift of grace that you can't earn hang in the balance like the team that depends on a last-second miracle kick to bail them out? *Don't depend on it.* Our God is unquestionably a merciful God, but there are stories in the Bible where God's patience ran out and he killed people. God killed Ananias and his wife for keeping part of the funds for the church. Only Noah and seven others were spared from the flood.

Are you determined to keep on sinning because there is pleasure in sin and expect a bailout after you have had your fun? After missing sign after sign to turn away from sin, are you going to wait for a deathbed miracle to save you? Your plan might be thwarted by your hardened heart. You might have a heart attack and die or you might fall into a coma and never have a chance to make the eternal game-changing decision. Your foot might slip, and you could wind up in a fatal car accident. God only gives us today, and the Bible makes it clear that you are a vapor, here today and gone tomorrow.

The odds grow longer with each passing decade that you will make that game-winning kick and come to know Christ. The winning kick gets more difficult, and the conditions seem to worsen, further stacking the odds against you. My brother in Christ, former pro wrestler Lex Luger, said to me, "We're single-digit guys." Lex meant that the odds of coming to know Christ after you are forty, as Lex and I did, are less than one in ten. I urge you to make the eternal, life-saving play the next time the Holy Spirit and God draw you to the Son. Then you can *know* you are victorious. As the final gun sounds to end your game on this earth, you can take the last snap, gracefully take a knee, raise your arms to the sky, and celebrate your victory in Jesus.

Prayer: Thank you for wooing me to your Son. Thank you for never giving up on my friends, my family members, and especially me. In Jesus's name, amen.

FB25:
EYE IN THE SKY

ISAIAH 55:8-9

For as the heavens are higher than the earth, so are my ways higher than your ways, and my thoughts are than your thoughts.

—Isaiah 55:9

On many football teams, the defensive and offensive coordinators sit in the press box high above the playing field. The better their view, the better their understanding is of the opponent's offensive and defensive schemes. The better their understanding of the schemes, the more likely that the coordinators will call the right plays. When you're at field level, the view is obscured because players are blocking your view of the game. It's difficult to see exactly where each player is positioned. If even one player's position is misunderstood, that mistake can result in a game-changing play and an easy touchdown for the opponent. Shouting and mass confusion on the sidelines distorts the coach's judgment. Sitting in the upper reaches of the press box provides an increased level of calm which results in better decision making.

NFL teams take Polaroid snapshots from high above the field of each play and fax them to the sideline. The faxed photos are placed in a three-ring binder. When the quarterback comes off the field, he can see each defensive formation from the previous drive. Those photos allow the quarterback to execute more effectively on the following drive.

God has the big picture. God has the eye in the sky and can see many things that you cannot see. You see the tip of the iceberg above the water, but God also sees the iceberg under the water. Would it not make complete sense to align with God, in effect, turn your life over to him since he knows what's coming and he knows what's best for your life? God loves you infinitely, and he already perfectly planned each day of the rest of your life. You won't be limited to your narrow, biased, myopic view of your circumstances in the world. Your personal power through Christ is unleashed when you are aligned with God's plan.

> Prayer: Father God, help me surrender my life to you so that I can unleash the mighty power that you can use through me. Help me trust you and remember that my thumbnail view of a situation can't hold a candle to your infinite knowledge. In Jesus's name, amen.

FB26:
TONY DUNGY

PHILIPPIANS 4:13

I can do all things through Christ who strengthens me.

After his Indianapolis Colts convincingly won Super Bowl XLI in 2007, Tony Dungy became the most respected coach in the NFL. Dungy soon retired from coaching. He became an NBC football analyst, but he also chose to spend more time making a difference for Jesus Christ. Dungy became the spokesman for All-Pro Dad, a nationwide program introduced by Family First with his help that teaches men how to become better fathers by living out Christian principles.

Notably, he mentored Philadelphia Eagles quarterback Michael Vick weekly when Michael was being held in a maximum security prison in Leavenworth, Kansas. Many people believe that he helped Vick discover his new life in Christ. With Dungy by his side, Vick testified of his newly discovered faith at a Super Bowl prayer breakfast in February 2010.

Coach Dungy once explained that "the Bible is life's playbook. It provides answers to the biggest questions life has. With the Colts, we have a playbook that details exactly what we want to do. If a player is uncertain, he only has to read the playbook. The Bible is like that. When we're not sure how to act, how to deal with a certain situation, we go to the Bible to get God's plan for how it should be done. Through his Son, Jesus Christ, God has revealed how we are to live."

> Prayer: Father God, thank you for the difference that a Christian brother such as Tony Dungy can make in the lives of other men. May I learn from his example of serving others, faith sharing, and discipleship. In Jesus's name, amen.

FB27:
MARK RICHT

JEREMIAH 29:11

I know the plans that I have for you, says the Lord. Plans
for your welfare and not for harm, to give you a future with
hope. (TLB)

Mark Richt has been the head football coach at the University of
Georgia since 2001. He has led the Dawgs to two SEC championships and several Top 5 rankings. Coach Richt is known for
his calm under pressure, his servant heart, and his willingness to
share his faith with audiences across the Southeast. In March
2009, Coach Richt and Tony Dungy announced the expansion of
All-Pro Dad into college football at a press conference in Athens,
Georgia. Here is Coach Richt's account of how he came to a saving relationship with Jesus Christ when he was a young coach at
Florida State University.

    I was into my second season (coaching) at FSU and thought
that I was doing fairly well, until one fateful day in September…
One of our players was shot and killed while attending a party…
Coach Bowden called a team meeting…[and] pointed to the
empty chair that was assigned to the fallen player, and talked
about death and his faith. He asked every one of us in the room
to look at the chair and then he asked, 'If that was you, do you
know where you would spend eternity?'" "I was a broken young

coach, so the next day, I went to see him. He took me through the gospel and explained what it meant to be a Christian...It was time. My life had not turned out like I planned. I understood how self-centered and prideful I was. I saw my sin revealed and the reality of God's love for me...Coach Bowden led me in a prayer that day, and I received God's mercy, forgiveness, and peace through what Christ had done for me. I understood that... I would (never) be good enough to earn God's love. It is a free gift. I left Coach Bowden's office a new man.

> Prayer: Father God, thank you so much for the godly example set by Coach Richt, a man in the national spotlight who has consistently demonstrated that Jesus Christ is first in his life. May I emulate Christ-like faith and grow in my love for you. In the holy and precious name of Jesus, amen.

FB28:
SHAUN ALEXANDER

PSALM 37:4

Delight yourself also in the Lord, and He shall give you the desires of your heart.

Shaun Alexander was an All-American running back at the University of Alabama during the 1996–1999 seasons. After setting numerous rushing records for the Crimson Tide, he became an All-Pro with the Seattle Seahawks and led the NFL in rushing one season. Shaun wore number 37 during his football career, and one of his favorite verses comes from Psalm 37.

Shaun was certainly blessed with as much wealth and fame as life has to offer. Yet he remarked that possessions aren't the most important things in his life.

"A rich man thinks of himself as being rich," Shaun says. "I just think of myself as being blessed. If I'm just blessed, then I'll go out and bless other people…Most kids don't know that they're supposed to be something awesome in this world, or they don't believe they can be. I play to help them understand that they are special."

Shaun has never been the one to do something just because everyone else is. "I'm always the oddball compared to everyone else," he says. "That's because I don't live by their rules. I go by God's rules."

Prayer: Father God, may I learn from Shaun's example that the true riches in life come from living by your rules and being a blessing to others. Help me remember that when I am a blessing to others, I receive a blessing in return. In Jesus's name, amen.

FB29:
HERSCHEL WALKER

PROVERBS 3:5-6

Trust in the Lord with all of your heart, and lean not on
your own understanding; In all your ways acknowledge
Him, and He shall direct your paths. (NIV)

At the University of Georgia, Herschel Walker set an NCAA
freshman rushing record and helped his team capture the 1980
national collegiate football title. He earned consensus All-
American honors three consecutive years and capped a sensational college career by earning the 1982 Heisman trophy in his
junior year. Walker was one of the top running backs in the pros,
gaining more all-purpose yards than anyone in professional football history, counting his NFL and USFL seasons.

"My message is always about how Christ is in everything,"
Walker said. "I talk about how on a dollar bill we have 'In God
We Trust,' yet we don't put our trust in him. I talk about how
we've taken religion out of everything. Let's put it back. And I
talk about believing in Christ and putting faith in him and seeing
where that takes you."

Prayer: Most holy and gracious God, may I put my trust in you today and take a stand for Christ, whether I am at home or with my friends. Help me learn from Herschel that trusting in Christ will lead me where I need to go. In Jesus's name, amen.

FB30:
A FINAL DADGUM TRIBUTE
TO BOBBY BOWDEN

JOHN 15:5

If a man remains in me, and I in him, he will bear much fruit; apart from me you can do nothing. (NIV)

Coach Bobby Bowden went out in style at the 2010 Gator Bowl as his Florida State Seminoles upset West Virginia to give Coach Bowden his thirty-fourth consecutive winning season at Florida State. About 350 of his former players were in Jacksonville to see his final game. His numbers defy description with 389 career wins, two national championships (could have been five except for field goal attempts that went wide right), twelve conference championships, and, his most incredible stat to me, fourteen consecutive top-five finishes in the polls.

Unquestionably, Florida State coach Bobby Bowden is one of the most successful college football coaches in history. But few people in the sports world have advanced the cause of Jesus Christ as this man has. For over fifty years, Bowden has accepted invitations to speak whenever and wherever he can, particularly to church groups and particularly when he is on the road with the team.

When Bobby was twenty-three, he really got the picture and re-dedicated his life to the Lord. He recalled, "As I came up, I thought that being good was being a Christian. I knew you had to join the church. I joined the church. I knew you had to be baptized. I was baptized. I thought that, plus being good, makes you a Christian.

"I finally realized that you are saved by grace. It's nothing that you did and nothing that you earned. Once I understood that, it made life simpler to me. Because, with understanding grace, it makes you want to do better. Nobody's perfect. I make mistakes every day."

The ESPN ticker often streams negative publicity about coaches. However, during Bowden's final game as head coach, we were able to enjoy three hours of fond memories and bask in the glow of what is right in college sports. The Florida State fans appreciate the wins, but they must surely appreciate even more the legacy of the man who led them to those victories. Bobby's lasting legacy is the fruit that he has borne for the kingdom of God through his grace, his faithful witness, and his perseverance.

Prayer: Most gracious Lord, it is so awesome to see that a man of Bobby Bowden's fame seeks to deflect the glory to you. May his ministry of teaching men about Jesus Christ continue to bear fruit. In Jesus's name, amen.

FB31:
BORN TO DIE

ISAIAH 7:14, 9:6; MICAH 5:2, LUKE 2:10-16

Today a Savior, who is Messiah the Lord, was born for you
in the city of David.

—Luke 2:11 (HCS)

The 2009 Georgia high school football season ended with five
schools crowned champions of their respective classifications.
Notably, Buford High School won its fifth championship of the
decade. Once, *Sports Illustrated* published a feature article about
the winningest teams in America and anointed Valdosta, Georgia,
as its Winnersville, USA.

A South Georgia town on I-75 near the Florida line, Valdosta
became famous under the tutelage of legendary coach Wright
Bazemore, who won fourteen state titles, more than any coach
in Georgia high school history. As is the case in thousands of
small towns from Georgia to Texas to California, high school
football is approached with religious fervor in Valdosta. The town
set the tone a generation ago when nurses at the local hospital began placing tiny gold-and-black footballs in the bassinets
of its newborn males. The expectation was clear that these boys
were to grow up to become Valdosta Wildcats and help bring
more championships to the town. Proud daddies would train the
boys at an early age to catch and run with the stuffed footballs

until the lads graduated to pee wee football for formal training in blocking and tackling. If a boy didn't make the high school team, he could still play in the band or become a team manager. All should be devoted to the cause of the Wildcats.

However, the demographics shifted about twenty years ago, and now Lowndes County High School has emerged as the more dominant power in the county. Perhaps parents choose between gold-and-black footballs and maroon-and-gray footballs now at the hospital.

I experienced a Christmas concert presented by the gifted Christian pianist and composer Stanton Lanier (stantonlanier. com), the founder of a nonprofit organization called Music to Light the World. Stanton uses videos to great effect as he presents his scripturally inspired compositions and provides inspirational CDs to cancer wards across the country. In his closing video, a golden silhouette line emerged from the manger and wound across the dark landscape to a cross on a hillside. Just as baby boys in Valdosta received a toy revealing an expectation to play football in their futures, the baby Jesus had a different reminder placed in the manger. God figuratively placed a cross inside the manger because from his earliest recollection as a child, Jesus understood that there was a cross in his future. Jesus knew he would fulfill the prophecies at the age of thirty-three by dying on the cross because you and I are sinners. Jesus knew that he was born to die, and he lived to demonstrate God's great mercy and grace daily. Yes, Jesus was born to die but also to be raised from the grave on the third day.

Jesus beat death forever. Today, you can beat death by turning away from your sins and receiving Christ into your life. Jesus was born to die for your sins so that you can have eternal life in heaven, eternal life that begins the moment you prepare him a permanent place in your heart. This fundamental truth is the hope that all people can have, no matter what their circumstances might be. If you are a believer, share your hope with someone who desperately needs it.

Prayer: Father God, thank you for your immeasurable love that you would send your beloved Son, Jesus Christ, to be born as a baby. He came to walk among us, love us, and experience our hurts and disappointments and took our sins to the cross of Calvary so that we could be born again. May I share my hope in Christ with others. In Jesus's holy name, amen.

FB32: TOMMY BOWDEN

ISAIAH 45:22

Let all the world look to me for salvation! For I am God, there is no other.

Tommy Bowden is the son of Bobby Bowden. Tommy was also a winning head football coach on the collegiate level at Tulane University and Clemson University. The Bowden family has long exemplified a deep-seated faith that has endured through success on the field, through adversity, and through the tragic loss of a grandson. Tommy wrote the following poem, which speaks of gratitude and Christian principles that we can use to guide us through each day.

> Guide and strengthen us through each day, to act and talk in a Christ-like way.
> Though we are not worthy of his awesome power, we need it to survive each and every hour.
> Boy, it is great to have a God to love, Who's always there, just right above.
> A God so great, He gave his only Son, Yes, for me, you, and everyone.
>
> —Excerpt from "A Simple Call,"
> Tommy Bowden, 1973

Prayer: Most gracious and loving God, thank you for your immeasurable, incomparable, unfathomable, infinite love, which you demonstrated so incredibly through the death and resurrection of Jesus. Thank you, Father, for your peace which passes understanding that is available to each person who knows Jesus as Savior and Lord. In the precious name of our Savior, the One who took our place, amen.

FB33:
BUYIN' OR SELLIN'? NEED ONE!

MATTHEW 7:13

Heaven can only be entered through the narrow gate!
(TLB)

I have found tickets for a World Series game in Kansas City, the Georgia–Florida game, the football national championship game in New Orleans, and the basketball Final Four in Atlanta. My keys are to arrive several hours in advance, find a high-traffic area away from the stadium, dress well, be polite, put two fingers in the air, and have my cash ready. Eventually, a non-scalper will offer to sell you tickets. Finding one ticket is easier than finding two and much easier than finding four.

If you're really desperate, have your daughter stand on the street with the "Need Masters Badges" sign she made and say, "Look as pitiful as possible." On Sunday afternoon of the 2001 Masters, a man in a car pulled over and said, "Is that your daughter (Allison) down there with the sign? She sure looks sad. I have a couple of badges I'm willing to sell you." My daughters Allison (Georgia–Auburn, 2002) and Jillian (Georgia–Florida, 2007) have learned to fend for themselves. I tease them that Becca taught them most things they need to know, but Dad taught them how to buy tickets.

In the upcoming anecdote, I want to be perfectly clear that I do not condone my behavior and actions. The only reason I got away with it is that security was pretty lax in 1982. I could have been arrested and fined several hundred dollars for improper possession of a football ticket and resisting arrest by running, which would have been quite embarrassing for me and my wife.

One time, I didn't follow my keys. In 1982, number-one-ranked Georgia played at Auburn. Becca and I drove down with Joel and Marlene. But we got there later than intended. There was no TV and perfect weather, which made tickets really scarce. A friend sold us two tickets at face, but at game time, we were still two short. We weren't prepared for this scenario, so the ladies chilled, and Joel and I kept looking. Midway through the first quarter, an Auburn student inside the stadium slipped me an Auburn faculty pass through the chain-link fence for $20. I went through the pass gate with no problem, handed the faculty pass to Joel through the fence, and he got in. Yes! We celebrated with a leaping high five, and security saw us. I was empty-handed, so I took off running. I finally reunited with Becca before halftime in the Georgia section. The game was almost an afterthought. Georgia won 19–14 to qualify for the Sugar Bowl after Auburn tight end Ed West tripped over the Georgia twenty-yard line, and Georgia hunkered down for a last-minute stand. Georgia announcer Larry Munson yelled, "Oh, look at the sugar falling from the sky!" and an Auburn fan threw a drink in his face.

Obviously, we took quite a risk going to the game with no tickets. We worked very hard to get inside. Since it was a faculty pass, only through the pass gate could I enter. If the ticket taker had denied me, two of us would have never seen the game.

Please realize that I broke the Ten Commandments by lying, coveting, and stealing. You should never try what I did.

One-Way Complimentary Ticket
Site: Heaven
Gate: Pearly
Price: Paid in Full by Christ

Make sure you have secured your ticket to heaven. You are at risk if you haven't done it. You can work hard, but you cannot earn one. No matter how rich you are, there won't be any tickets for buyin' and sellin' outside heaven's gate because Jesus purchased all tickets at the cross. There is only one gate, the pearly gates, where you can enter. To secure your ticket to enter heaven, you need to repent, which means to turn away from your sinful life, ask for forgiveness, and place your trust in Christ. Then you'll see the greatest game ever.

> Prayer: Most holy and gracious Father God, thank you for the excitement and pleasure that I get from attending sporting events. May I always keep these contests in perspective and thank you for forgiving me when I lose it. Thank you for purchasing my ticket to heaven. In Jesus's name, amen.

FB34:
EVER FEEL LIKE VANDY?

ROMANS 8:18

What we suffer now is nothing compared to the glory we
will receive later. (TLB, paraphrased)

Vanderbilt University is one of the elite academic institutions in
America, but Vandy has traditionally been the football doormat
of the SEC. Since the creation of the Southeastern Conference
in 1933, Vandy is the only charter member still in the conference that has never won or even shared the SEC football title.
The odds that Vandy will win the SEC next season are probably
five hundred to one. The school eliminated its athletic director in
2003 and placed the athletic department under the vice chancel-
lor of the Department of Student Life and University Affairs.
Vandy's stadium is rarely full and is half the capacity of seven
of the schools in the conference, so Vandy will never truly have
a home field advantage. Due to its higher academic standards,
Vandy will never get the same athletes as most of the schools in
the SEC, especially the half-dozen elite programs. A great season
at Vandy is getting to any bowl game. A great record at Vandy
could get you fired at an elite SEC school. Vandy went to its first
bowl game in twenty-five years in 2008. That's a tremendous year
at Vandy. The odds are simply stacked against the 'Dores being

a consistent winner. The occasional upset that Vandy achieves makes it worthwhile to keep playing in the league.

Does your life ever feel like you're trying to compete against a stacked deck like Vandy? Maybe it's because your job isn't going well and you're the lowest person in your team's ratings. Perhaps you're struggling to make your grades as a student. It could be an uphill battle trying to make the varsity team or saving to pay for a car while your friend gets a new one. Maybe it's failing health or the health of a loved one that has you on the treadmill that never seems to stop.

Whatever your challenge, relish in the fact that you've made it this far. Relish in the fact that God wants to help you through any situation that you encounter. God gives us today, and God never takes a day off. Occasionally, I say a short prayer as I approach the revolving glass doors of my office building. It goes like this: "God, give me the strength to make it through today." Nine hours later, I walk through those same doors and don't remember what I was so concerned about. God always delivers. His mercy is great, and his grace is even greater. Remember to celebrate the blessings and victories that you and God have achieved together, and know that your rewards for perseverance, loyalty, and simply having the courage to show up each day and battle will be great in heaven.

> Prayer: Most gracious Lord, you have come through for me so many times when the deck seems stacked against me. I appreciate you always being there and never leaving nor forsaking me. In Jesus's holy and precious name, amen.

FB35:
TAKE A KNEE

PHILIPPIANS 2:8-11

Every knee shall bow,…and every tongue shall confess that Jesus Christ is Lord…

—Philippians 2:10-11

One of the most joyous moments for a football fan is when your team's defense has prevented a last-gasp scoring drive and your offense takes over on downs. Your team has a four-point lead, there are forty-five seconds remaining, and the opposing defense has no timeouts. You shout, "There's no way we can lose!" Many years ago, the quarterback would hand off to the running back to plunge into the line. But the New York Giants changed that approach in 1978 by losing a game to the Philadelphia Eagles in the last thirty seconds. Quarterback Joe Pisarcik (Giants fans just groaned at the sight of that name) fumbled an exchange to full-back Larry Csonka, and defensive back Herm Edwards picked up the loose ball and rambled twenty-five yards for a touchdown. That was a big ouch.

Ever since that play, teams take absolutely no chances. Before the ball is snapped, the entire offensive team forms a shell around the quarterback to protect him even further. The quarterback takes a direct snap from center and kneels immediately. By taking a knee, the quarterback stops the play and cannot be tackled.

The quarterback might take a knee two or three times to run out the clock. After the last knee is taken and the play clock has more seconds than the game clock, it's time for the coach's Gatorade bath as players pour onto the field to shake hands.

The Bible makes it clear that all will honor Christ when he comes back on a white horse to establish his rule on this earth as prophesied in the book of Revelation. Philippians tells us that one day, everyone in heaven, on earth, and under the earth will take a knee when Christ returns. Every knee will bow, and every tongue will proclaim that Jesus Christ is Lord. His second coming and the symbolic taking of the knee will signify that the New Ruler of the earth, Jesus Christ, has won the eternal victory over Satan. When you take a knee, give thanks to God for the prophecy and his perfect plan to return Christ to the site of his victory over death.

> Prayer: Dear Father, when I take a knee tonight before I go to bed, I will thank you for Jesus and his impending victory over Satan's forces here on earth. In Jesus's holy name, amen.

FB36:
THE GATORADE BATH

LUKE 3:21-22, EPHESIANS 4:30

And the Holy Spirit descended in bodily form like a dove upon Him…

—Luke 3:22

Invariably, the winning head football coach receives the traditional Gatorade bath at the end of the game. According to the *Atlanta Journal-Constitution*, the Gatorade bath originated when New York Giants OG Jim Burt doused Head Coach Bill Parcells after a game. Apparently, Burt teased Parcells all week at practice that he would soak him if the Giants won. Now, I'm a cold-natured person, and I don't like cold showers at all. I won't take a cold shower unless there is no alternative. My first thank-you of the day to God is sometime in the first five seconds of that soothing hot water hitting my back. So when I see two burly linemen carrying the bucket of ice-laden colored liquid to dump it on an unsuspecting coach, I cringe, especially when the temperature on the field is colder than the water. Dumping an icy torrent of Gatorade seems appropriate for a young coach on an eighty-degree day, but when you dump it on an old coach on a cold day, that's insane. The winning coach gets the icy bath. Why not dump the Gatorade bucket on the loser?

It's also dangerous. My wife, Becca, recalled that Long Beach State Head Coach George Allen, seventy-two, formerly of the Washington Redskins, received an ice-cold water dousing in 1990 from his overzealous Long Beach State football team. Unfortunately, Coach Allen came down with pneumonia and died six weeks later, and the dousing may have been a contributing factor to his decline. Maybe Gatorade baths are one reason that head coaches make the big bucks.

So we see these coaches being baptized with Gatorade. The effect on their nervous systems must literally take their breath away. The Holy Spirit comes upon you in a different way when you receive Christ. The same Holy Spirit that you and I received also descended bodily upon Jesus just after he was baptized in the River Jordan. I wonder how cold that water was. You are changed forever when you are bathed in the Holy Spirit. It doesn't feel like the Gatorade bath, thank goodness. When you are bathed in the Holy Spirit, you are sealed for eternity. What is God going to do if you sin? Because you will still sin. He's not going to reach down and yank the Holy Spirit out of your body like you've got on a cheap shirt because you have been sealed for eternity with the Holy Spirit. God says to Satan, "This one is mine! You can never take this one away from me." Soon, you will observe that the worldly things that drove you to distraction no longer have the same hold on you because that is Living Water flowing through your body.

Envision the Gatorade bath after an upset of your archrival washing away the frustration of a losing season. In a similar fashion, the baptism of the Holy Spirit washes away the frustrations of trying do it all by yourself your whole life. Now you will learn to allow God to lead you and direct your life. Being cleansed by the blood of Jesus Christ is imperative for salvation, and the Holy Spirit is God's way of putting the icing on the cake. It's a gift that only God can pour on you and into you.

Prayer: Most gracious and loving God, please pour out your mercies, blessings, and grace upon me. I am grateful for every single gift you give me. And I'm especially appreciative of the Holy Spirit, the gift that seals me for eternity in you and with you. In Jesus's name, amen.

FB37:
IS GOD NUMBER ONE THIS WEEK IN YOUR POLL?

ISAIAH 42:8; 44:6, 8; 45:5, 22

I am the Lord, and there is no other. There is no God besides me.

—Isaiah 45:5

Alabama was crowned 2009 national champs by virtue of their 37–21 BCS Championship Game win over Texas. For all of the passionate Alabama and Texas fans who returned from Pasadena, their reentry into the real world in the middle of January must have been difficult, especially for the Texas fans.

Certainly you must appreciate the fans who avidly support their teams. However, passion overdone can leave a person in a deep funk, even withdrawal, when his or her team loses. Fandom that becomes idol worship is something each sports fan must guard against or else God will be displaced from his number-one ranking.

Speaking of number one, if you were to rank your passions from week to week, how many weeks would God occupy the top spot in your life? There are your favorite teams, your favorite athletes, blogs, Internet, TV, selfish pursuits, work, and school.

All of these god-isms vie for top spot in your life. Think about the number of hours you spent on each activity when you don't consciously include God. It's easy to give God the top spot each Sunday morning, but by Sunday evening, has he slipped in your poll? How about Thursday night after you've slogged through a difficult week as the world has tried to drag you through the mire with work and school challenges and family problems? How about any strongholds that Satan has used to separate you from God and shove him further down your poll?

If you asked your closest friends, family members, and coworkers to vote and be perfectly truthful, how many first-place votes would God really get compared to first-place votes for the *I* team (me, myself, and I)? God can easily be knocked off the top rung if you allow yourself to lose focus on him. It has happened to me with Georgia football, Kentucky basketball, golf, and too much TV and Internet. Once God drops to number two behind your self-interests and idolatry, your kingdom work ceases.

Beware of Satan's toehold because the toehold can become a foothold, which can become a stronghold, which can become an entire possession. Daily perspective gained through prayer and reading the Bible, which helps us be more obedient to God, is essential to keep God number one in our weekly poll. Otherwise, we unconsciously give Satan the top spot, which is like your team's bitter rival pulling an upset. If we realize it is Satan we've allowed to climb to the top, we'll fight harder to defeat the stronghold and put God back in his proper position.

> Prayer: Father God, help me take a daily checkpoint and realize when I'm focused on something that has taken your place. Please, Lord, help me to always keep you at the top. In Jesus's name, amen.

FB38:
COLT MCCOY EXHIBITS GOD'S GRACE IN DEFEAT

JOB 1:13–2:10

> Shall we receive good at the hand of God, and shall we not receive evil?
>
> —Job 2:10

Alabama defeated Texas 37–21 for the 2009 BCS football national championship. Colt McCoy, Texas's Heisman candidate and quarterback, was knocked out on the sixth play from scrimmage on a hit he had taken many times before. Though Texas fought bravely, Bama's running game and ball-hawking defense proved to be too much to overcome.

After the game, Colt McCoy was interviewed by Lisa Salters, the ABC sideline reporter. She immediately asked him a point-blank question about how it felt to get hurt and miss winning the national championship. Colt took five to ten seconds to collect himself emotionally, and his answer was replete with humility, grace, and gratitude. For a young man who saw his dreams of winning a national championship taken away when he was forced to the sidelines, it was a demonstration of tremendous character.

First, he made sure that he gave Alabama credit and congratulated them on a great game. Second, despite the outcome, Colt said, "I always give God the glory. I'd never question why things happen the way they do. God is in control...I know I'm standing on the Rock." It reminded me so much of Job when Job's wife told him that he should curse God and die after the calamities struck. But Job's response was that he gave God the glory when things were going great, and he was going to give God the glory now when things were going bad. Colt said that he would still exalt God in his disappointment and sadness. Third, he told the national TV audience that he had a dead arm from the hit. Here was a young man with a chance to be drafted in the first or second round telling the NFL scouts the truth about exactly what happened.

I was totally moved by the grace that Colt demonstrated. Without the injury, Colt might not have had the platform to make such a moving statement, and he took full advantage of it for the kingdom. Hallelujah and to God be the glory, honor, and praise.

> Prayer: Father God, thank you for the Christian example of Colt McCoy and so many young athletes who recognize their opportunities to give you the glory and to honor you with praise. May I take advantage of the chances that I have to share my faith eloquently and passionately. In Jesus's holy name, amen.

FB39:
THE RIGHT PLAY
AT THE RIGHT TIME

ZEPHANIAH 3:17, 1 CORINTHIANS 9:22, JOHN 3:30

I am made all things to all men, that I might by all means save some.

—1 Corinthians 9:22 (KJV)

College football is no longer "three yards and a cloud of dust." The athletes are too fast and too strong, and the coaching is too sophisticated. Plus, football tickets need to be sold to pay the bills for all of the interscholastic sports. There are hundreds of possible offensive plays and defensive formations. Intense film study into the wee hours pays off when a play is discovered that will score against a particular defense on a particular down and yardage situation.

I Googled the scoring drive with the most plays in history. Against New Mexico in the 2004 Emerald Bowl, Navy reeled off an incredible twenty-six-play, ninety-four-yard scoring drive that lasted almost fifteen minutes. Consider there are at least twenty-six different ways to score TDs: QB sneak, bomb, corner, post, post corner, hook and ladder, sprint draw, down and out, QB draw, wildcat, off tackle, sweep, tunnel screen, screen pass, fumblerooski, slant, end around, reverse, double reverse, tackle eligible, tailback hurdles the line, flea flicker, Statue of Liberty, fade, running back pass, and buttonhook. Most football fans would agree that each of these twenty-six plays has produced many touchdowns. The key is to call the right play at the right time.

God has an infinite number of plays in his playbook that he can call to score for his kingdom. Here are twenty-six different ways God uses to bring people to Christ: sermons, the Word, intercessory prayer, spiritual pamphlets, mission trips, devotions, VBS, Young Life, evangelists, revivals, Kairos prison ministry, parents, grandparents, confirmation class, FCA, sports ministries, Christian music, personal testimonies, Christian movies, Sunday school, relationship building, Gideon Bibles, youth retreats, youth group, lay speakers, family reunions, and last but not least, good deeds in the name of Christ. Oops. That's twenty-seven. Most Christians would agree that God has used each method to produce many scores (conversions or new believers).

One key is to follow God's guidance and employ an appropriate method that is consistent with God's timing. God always "gives the increase" (John 3:30), which means that only God brings people into his kingdom, but we are his hands, feet, and spokespersons. My good friend, Dr. George Morris, senior professor of World Evangelism of the World Methodist Council, shared the following quote by William Barclay: "God has his own secret stairway into every heart." A person can have significant spiritual experiences and influences over a lifetime. Then comes the game-breaking special occasion in a person's life that breaks the bondage of sin for eternity through Jesus Christ.

As Christians, it is our duty to sow seeds and shine our light in prayerful expectation that many will receive Christ as Savior and Lord. Sometimes, our faith sharing is the first play in a person's fifteen-play faith drive. It could be the fourth play or the eighth play. Occasionally, we experience the thrill of the last play that catapults a person into Christ's end zone. All of the plays contribute, but it's the final seed sown at the right time that pays off.

I believe that as Christians, we must be open to various approaches. To say, "That way doesn't work. You must use this way," puts God in a box. As the heavens are higher than the earth, his ways are greater than our ways (Isaiah 55:9). Only God knows how many hearts are changed using a particular approach. When Paul taught us to reach people by all means, I believe that he meant use every good and holy way at our disposal. Discernment means understanding which approach to use, how to use it, and when to use it. God has incomparably great power, and God is mighty to save. Yet he chose flawed human beings to spread the good news. Unfortunately, we sometimes stumble when we try to tell people what Jesus means to us, but it still pleases God when we make the attempt. I read that an evangelist once said that he would always choose sharing the gospel imperfectly over someone else not trying. God uses his children's efforts every day to push people over heaven's goal line.

> Prayer: Most wonderful and creative God of the universe, open my eyes wide that I may see there is more than one way to "skin a cat." Thank you for the incredible variety of ways that you have given us to share the gospel. In Jesus's name, amen.

FB40:
COMING OFF THE BENCH

MATTHEW 11:28, 27:32

And they compelled one Simeon, a Cyrenean who passed by, coming out of the country, the father of Alexander and Rufus, to bear his cross.

—Matthew 27:32 (KJV)

Certainly, there are times when athletes unexpectedly enter important contests. Garrett Gilbert, a freshman quarterback at the University of Texas, was thrust into the glare of the national spotlight in the 2009 BCS Championship Game. He had only appeared in mop-up roles behind Colt McCoy, Heisman Trophy finalist and the winner of more FBS games than any quarterback ever. But suddenly, Colt went down with a shoulder injury, the first significant setback of his career, in his final game. Fortunately, Garrett performed admirably. After a rough first half against the nation's top defense that included a pick six on the final play, Garrett settled down and threw two touchdown passes and kept Texas in the game until the final few minutes. He had a chance to lead his team to victory before a blindside sack ended the Longhorns' hopes.

Almost two thousand years before, a man named Simeon and his two sons had no idea what they were in for when they awoke one morning. Amid the hustle and bustle of Jerusalem packed with people for Holy Week, Simeon wondered, *What's all the shouting about, and what's with this cadre of Roman centurions?* One of the centurions pulled Simeon from the crowd into the Via Dolorosa and ordered him to carry a cross. Simeon thought, *Who is this man, savagely beaten, bleeding profusely, bruised, gasping for air, in excruciating pain, yet no complaints come from his lips?*

You want me do what? Simeon surely thought. *And what about my sons?*

The Roman guard yelled, "Do as you're told, and don't ask questions! Help him carry this cross! Just do it!"

The man was Simeon of Cyrene, and he certainly never expected to become a part of the story. He was a bit player in the midst of the most important event in history. Simeon did as he was instructed and helped Jesus drag that cross up a hill named Golgotha, where Jesus would be nailed to the cross while carrying our past, present, and future sin with him.

You and I can suddenly be thrust into the spotlight and have no choice but to play an unexpected role in the game of life. A family member could become ill, and you might need to take a part-time job to help out financially. This additional responsibility could place stress on you as you try to keep up your grades. A knee injury could derail your dreams of a college scholarship. Your friends could drop you because you chose to take a stand for Christ. But through a close relationship with God, you can rely on him to see you through any difficulty that you may encounter.

As Simeon helped Jesus shoulder his cross, God will help you shoulder your daily trials. His yoke is easy. Give him your burdens and cares. God will help you dig deep and find the faith to keep from losing it. No matter what life might throw at you, God is there to give you strength, perseverance, grit, and hope to help you handle stress and strain like a saint. Now is the time to build your reserves through daily walks with God that include gratitude, Bible study, and prayer. Without the daily walks, we are ill-prepared when trials come.

Prayer: Father God, you are so merciful and gracious to me. Help me realize that every day, you want to sit with me and talk with me and walk with me. When those stormy days happen and I really need you, I will come to you out of habit developed by love, not out of desperation. In Jesus's holy name, amen.

FB41:
THE ICING ON THE CAKE

MATTHEW 6:33

Seek first the Kingdom of God and his righteousness, and
all these things shall be added to you.

UGA's Drew Butler is the son of Kevin Butler, the former Georgia
All-American and College Hall of Fame place kicker. Drew was
signed as a punter and place kicker, but he didn't resemble a chip
off the old block during his first two seasons on campus. He was
the backup punter as a redshirt freshman and was no threat to
erase his dad's kicking records. "He got a scholarship because
of his daddy!" some cried. But when the punting job opened up
the following season, Butler was ready. Man, was he ready. He
consistently boomed high punts and placed them beautifully,
especially against Arkansas when his seventy-five-yard kick from
scrimmage sealed the victory. For the season, Drew averaged an
astounding forty-nine yards per punt, which was four yards more
than a trio of kickers who were distant in the rearview mirror. Four
yards might not sound like much, but that margin on the PGA
Tour would be like driving the ball twenty-five yards farther than
your closest competitors. His father, Kevin, commented that his
consistently good punts were his outstanding accomplishment.

Through excellent technique, thorough mental preparation, and through a newfound passion for punting, Drew achieved great success. The postseason awards rolled in by the bushel basket. There was the Walter Camp Award, the Ray Guy Award, and numerous first-team All-American honors. But the awards were not what Drew set out to achieve. His singular focus was to become the best punter he could be and win the starting position at UGA. As a result of his hard work and excellence, the postseason accolades were the icing on the cake.

Jesus taught us in the book of Matthew that you and I are to put first things first. Seek first God's kingdom and his righteousness by being a daily disciple devoted to right living with fervent focus on prayer, Bible study, love for God, and obedience. A self-righteous person will perform good works and say as the Pharisees said, "Look at me! Look what I've done!" That selfish attitude won't get you special blessings from God. But a person who receives God's special favor is the one who gives God the glory no matter what comes out of situations. That's when God pours out the whipped cream and the cherry on top. Those blessings can be unexpected, wonderful compliments from a Christian brother or sister or special opportunities that God grants you. It could be a kind word when you need it most from a friend who saw your light shine for Christ. First things first. Jesus, then others, then yourself spells J-O-Y, joy.

> Prayer: Father God, help me to work hard not simply for the pats on the back, which are cool, but because I have a mindset and a heart set on serving you. Not because of what I've done, but because of what you've done for me. Not because of who I am, but because of who you are. In Jesus's name, amen.

FB42:
SOLD OUT!

2 CORINTHIANS 11:23-28, PHILIPPIANS 1:20-21, 3:8; JAMES 1:2-4

For to me to live is Christ, and to die is gain.

—Philippians 1:21

A sellout means all tickets have been sold and none remain. A sellout crowd adds another level of excitement to a sports contest when you look around and realize that there are virtually no empty seats. The only thing better than a sellout is SRO, standing room only, which is beyond capacity. Nothing pleases a team's marketing director like a sellout. The Masters wouldn't be the same if you could walk up and buy badges the day of the tournament. Successful teams that routinely sell out publish the same attendance figure. Sanford Stadium's published capacity is 92,746. Nebraska has sold out 190 consecutive games dating back to the 1970s, when coaches Bob Devaney and Tom Osborne put the Huskers on the national map. A sellout can make finding tickets a real adventure.

God loves sellouts too. He can't get enough of them. But a sellout to God is when a person consistently gives God 100 percent in each facet of their lives. Too many Christians settle for partial sellouts, which aren't nearly as exciting. A partial sellout is when a person holds back certain parts of their lives. That's no sellout at all.

God wants complete surrender to maximize a person's value to his kingdom. When you sell out to God, he will maximize his blessings to you. That doesn't mean you'll get rich monetarily or never have problems, but you will have a special coping strength that others do not have.

A person who is sold out to God doesn't take days off. A person who is sold out to God thinks about eternity virtually every day. He or she goes out the door in the morning expecting to see opportunities to share God's love and to expand the kingdom. A person who is sold out to God will find where God is working and join him there. A person who is sold out to God doesn't need to be reminded that there is kingdom work to be done. A person who is sold out to God illumines the Holy Spirit. Know any sellouts?

When newspapers and websites publish box scores, the attendance figures are shared, and the capacity of the stadium is shown in parentheses. For example, "15,370 (20,468)" indicates that there were over five thousand empty seats for the contest. How would your actual contributions compare to your capacity to contribute if God were to reveal it? Would it be 25 percent or 100 percent most days? Which is closer to your true measure?

Certainly Paul was sold out to God. He counted everything that he had experienced or possessed to be dung or manure when compared to knowing Christ. Only a sellout could have endured so many mental and physical hardships and stayed steadfast in promoting the good news of the resurrection and the love of Jesus Christ. Paul sold out to Christ because Christ first sold out for Paul on the cross. We love because Christ first loved us.

Would you love to have joy even in the darkest tribulation? James 1:2 says, "Count it all joy when you fall into various trials." I can't tell you that I understand it, but I've seen it. I saw it when my friend, Melinda, told the estimated eight hundred people at her daughter's funeral that if any of them didn't know Jesus Christ, she wanted to talk to them after the service. Surrendering and selling out to Christ is the only way to true joy. Otherwise, you are settling for second best. Selling out to God adds excitement to your life. What a difference it will make if you approach each day with an eternal focus.

Prayer: Lord Jesus, thank you for selling out for me on the cross. I can never repay you, but I can think about you each day and try to live my life as a disciple of Christ should live. May you help me in that endeavor each day with the strength and courage that I need to succeed not as the world sees success but as you see it. In Jesus's name, amen.

FB43:
PROPHETIC
PROGNOSTICATIONS

DANIEL 9:24-27, REVELATION 20:11-21:5

And I saw a great white throne, and Him that sat on it…

—Revelation 20:11 (KJV)

Think of all the talking TV suits, the panel of so-called sports experts who spend hour upon hour on pregame shows, picking the winners of games. I saw seven ESPN experts pick the NFC and AFC championship games. They were a combined one game above 50 percent picking winners in the previous NFL playoff games. That percentage is the same as flipping a coin.

Consider your emotional reaction when an expert picks your favorite team to win. It gives you a false sense of confidence that is shaken thirty seconds later when another prognosticator picks your archrival to win. You seethe a little at that guy and say he is biased. And, of course, he doesn't know what he's talking about, does he?

The spectacle of game predictions and expert advice can be pretty comical. I heard one basketball pundit, an ex-college and pro player, say before the Kentucky–Florida basketball game that "Florida needs to employ their running game to beat Kentucky."

When Florida was down twelve at the half, the same guy says, "Florida can't afford to get into a running game." I couldn't make those two statements up, the second of which was a correction of his misinformed assertion one hour before. Then there are the talking heads on ESPN who always pick opposite each other.

At one time in my young Christian life, I disrespected the teachings of the Old Testament by thinking that the New Testament was all that was needed since we are saved by faith through Jesus Christ. What does it really matter what happened before Christ was born as long as we have Christ? But as I delved into the Old Testament, I became enamored with the prophecies, particularly those that predicted the birth, life, death, and resurrection of Jesus. The odds that so many prophecies would come true are staggering, approaching 10^{132} according to Lee Strobel, who authored *The Case for Christ*. Those are incomprehensibly huge odds, because 10^9 power is a billion to one!

God bats one hundred percent in his predictions, unlike the flip-a-coin prognosticators. Not only that, but God's timing is perfect. Consider the prophecy of Daniel (9:24–27) that predicted almost five hundred years earlier the exact day that Jesus would humbly and triumphantly enter Jerusalem on a colt as the crowds cheered, "Hosanna in the highest!"

Unlike other religions, Christianity is the only religion with the element of proven prophecies, hundreds of them, and the only religion that worships a risen savior. All others trace their roots back to people who were of this earth. Jesus came from beyond this earth to be born to a virgin. The sheer amount of evidence of proven prophecies ought to be enough to silence the greatest naysayers.

There are some big prophecies remaining in the book of Revelation. These predictions will come true in God's timing. As revealed to the writer John as he was exiled on the isle of Patmos, the Great White Throne Judgment, the lake of fire, and the second coming of Jesus will occur. I would never pick against God, and neither should you.

He is the incomparably great and mighty Most Holy God that we serve. If it's between God and Satan for the second coming, I'm taking God, who will be the favorite to win every time. You and I must have unshakable faith that God will do what he said he would do.

> Prayer: Most Holy and magnificent Father, you are perfect, and your Word is perfect. I believe that what you say has happened and will happen even though I don't understand all of the events. May I live my life like Jesus will be on my doorstep later today. In Jesus's holy and precious name, amen.

FB44:
STAY UNTIL THE END

MATTHEW 27:38-43

And they that passed by reviled him, wagging their heads.

—Matthew 27:39 (KJV)

Let's admit it. Many of us take great pleasure in seeing our archrivals lose to us. In the SEC, if you are a visiting fan, be prepared to take some ribbing. Unfortunately, the ribbing can become taunting and meanness from some unruly fans. It's enough to make you want to leave the stadium early. Oftentimes, that's exactly what happens. You're on the road, and things turn against your team from the start. Then you're down three touchdowns and the opponent punches in one more just for good measure. As soon as the official lifts his hands to signal touchdown, it starts. "I've seen enough. Let's go." "Let's beat the traffic." "He [the coach] has gotta go." "I can't believe I wasted my money to come here." Before the extra point sails through the goal posts, the visiting section of the stands is empty. "Hey, hey, goodbye!" is one of the milder chants that goes up. "See you! Wouldn't wanna be you!" Your only goal is to get to your car in the parking lot, load up, beat the traffic, and set sail for home because visions of an undefeated season have gone up in smoke. And it's only October.

Imagine how your team feels when their fans abandon them after they have played their hearts out. They can't help but see it, especially if it's the home crowd that leaves in droves. Then the visiting fans take great delight when the vast majority of the stadium exits. These circumstances have an interesting parallel to what Jesus experienced in the final hours on the cross. Many of the chief priests, scribes, elders, and the Roman soldiers took great pleasure in seeing Jesus "get his." After all, Jesus had been a major thorn in their sides for three years. The air at Golgotha was filled with taunting and meanness. "If you're the Son of God, save yourself! Come down from the cross!" they cried with glee. It was enough to make the disciples of Jesus flee the scene early. Things had suddenly turned against them, and they ran like scared rabbits. Even Peter, who had vowed hours before that he would be faithful to the end, denied Jesus three times just as Jesus had predicted, and the cock crowed. The only followers of Jesus left were the Apostle John, his mother, Mary, another Mary, and Salome. Jesus had virtually no other followers in the stands, and he still had several hours remaining in the longest game of his life.

Imagine how Jesus felt when his disciples abandoned him, and their sins had helped put him on the cross. After Jesus turned what was seemingly the worst loss ever into the greatest victory for mankind, these same eleven would become the greatest spokespersons for Christianity after receiving the power of the Holy Spirit. Today, Christians can take great delight in the hope, peace, joy, and eternal life that only Jesus Christ brings.

> Prayer: Father God, before I leave the stadium, help me consider how my team feels when I abandon them in their time of need. Jesus, I never want to turn my back on you when the going gets tough because you never turned your back on me. You hung to make me strong, to help me endure and bounce back for another day. In Jesus's name, amen.

FB45:
I'M IN THE BATHROOM
'CAUSE THERE'S NO PLACE
FOR ME TO SIT!

LUKE 2:10-16

And they came with haste, and found Mary, and Joseph,
and the babe lying in a manger.

—Luke 2:16 (KJV)

In 2003, UGA football was coming off its best season in twenty
years, having won the SEC in 2002 and having finished in the
top five in the nation. Optimism was high; UGA was undefeated
and headed for an SEC showdown with LSU in Baton Rouge
in late September. I scraped together four single tickets for our
family before we left Atlanta. Allison was a second year at UGA,
and Jillian was a high school sophomore.

As I read the *Baton Rouge Advocate* on Saturday morning in
the hotel lobby while the three ladies got ready, it became obvious
that this was not just another game. The sportswriter touted the
contest as the biggest in Baton Rouge since 1963. *Man, am I glad
that we have tickets, even if they are singles,* I thought and breathed

a sigh of relief. *Surely Allison and Jillian can sit together since theirs are on the same row and only four seats apart.*

As we headed for the stadium, there were no tickets anywhere, so the stands would be jam-packed. We sorted through our game plan. Becca and I were in the same section about ten rows apart, so we could at least see each other even if we couldn't sit together. I helped Allison and Jillian find their section and encouraged them to ask people to let them sit together. But the people on that row were not very pleasant, so they never sat together. To make matters worse, when Jillian returned to her seat, two large male LSU fans were sitting in their seats and had consumed hers.

I found out her predicament just after kickoff as a hostile Tiger Stadium was in an uproar. I checked my cell phone and read this desperate text from Jillian, "I'm in the bathroom 'cause there's no place for me to sit!" I dashed down the aisle and brought her to my seat on the back row of the lower level. I crouched behind her for three and a half hours, and we watched our Dawgs lose 17–10. The day's events made Jillian pull against LSU forever, and the experience caused her to feel overwhelmed, rejected, alone, and afraid.

When the baby Jesus was born, he didn't exactly have the best seat in the house, or even have a seat for that matter. The innkeeper had a sellout that night. Joseph and Mary were told that there was no room in the inn, so they made their way outside the inn (stadium) and found themselves outside in a stable (under the stadium). The humble circumstances of the birth were just the beginning as Jesus found himself shuttled to Egypt to escape Herod's massacre of newborns. Christ would be rejected in his home town of Nazareth. Jesus would even be rejected by his family and constantly faced rejection for the new values that he had brought from the Father. Considering what Jesus went through during his life, certainly Jesus knew exactly how a frightened, lonely teenager felt in the bowels of Tiger Stadium, hiding out in a bathroom with nowhere to go and no place to sit. He knows exactly how you feel when you are in circumstances that threaten to engulf you.

> Prayer: Father God, thank you for comforting us when we feel like outcasts with nowhere to turn and no place to sit. You've been through every uncomfortable situation that we can face and help us turn to you when we have nowhere else to go. In Jesus's name, amen.

Note: Before that Georgia–LSU game, I walked around the ancient Cow Palace arena where my idol, Pete Maravich, performed so many times and wondered what it must have been like to watch Pete play in that building. Six weeks after this game, after being disconsolate over Georgia's second loss of the season, on a Sunday night, I was saved for eternity after watching a video of Pete Maravich's testimony in my living room. I never saw my salvation coming.

FB46:
JAW-DROPPING ASTONISHMENT

JOHN 14:2-4

In my Father's house are many mansions; if it were not so,
I would have told you. I go to prepare a place for you.

—John 14:2

Jillian and her friend, Liz, drove to Jacksonville for their first
Georgia–Florida game in 2007. They arrived at the game site
without tickets early on Saturday morning and were thrilled
to find two tickets from two kindly UGA gentlemen who had
extras. They were overjoyed just to get into the stadium. If the
tickets had been for the worst seats in Alltel Stadium, it wouldn't
have mattered. But the biggest thrill came when they went into
the stadium. First, they entered through a fancy private suite with
all the trappings and comforts and discovered their seats were on
the 40, fourth row, behind the Bulldogs' bench.

Jillian called us and screamed, "This is the best game that I've
ever been to!"

I replied, "Well, Jillian, that's great, because the game hasn't
even started."

To top off the incredible experience, Georgia upset Florida
42–30 in the "Celebration Game" that will forever be remembered fondly by Jillian, Liz, and all UGA fans who were there.

It was a day that started with joy and ended with jaw-dropping astonishment.

Following the Last Supper, Jesus shared with his disciples in the upper room that he would go before them and prepare a place for them. That place would be a special mansion/room in heaven with God and Jesus. Imagine what your special room in heaven will look like. It's far nicer than we can possibly fathom! God knows every hair on your head and every innermost thought. God knows exactly what makes you tick. I believe he will prepare us a special place to live with him for eternity that matches us to a *T*. I can't wait to see mine, and I bet you can't wait either. I believe our home in heaven will be absolutely jaw dropping!

> Prayer: Father God, you know exactly what makes us tick and what we enjoy. Thank you that you would prepare a place for us in heaven that we will be thrilled and overjoyed to see! In Jesus's name, amen.

FB47:
YOU ARE A FIVE-STAR RECRUIT!

PSALM 139:1-14

I am fearfully and wonderfully made…

—Psalm 139:14

National signing day for the 2009 college football season was predictable with a few surprises. Fans gathered in anxious anticipation at major college campuses across America or checked the Internet for the latest signing news throughout the day. There were the usual last-minute defections, and according to Rivals. com, mostly the rich got richer. My head was already spinning from the shakeout of major college football coaches getting dismissed for allegedly mistreating players and bolting for greener pastures. One father said he and his son should have bought into the university instead of the coach before signing. The impact of signing day on the future of many young men was life changing.

The pressure on these teenagers and their parents to make life-altering decisions is enormous. Savvy recruiters have used their polished sales pitches and stretch limos, sat in basketball bleachers to be seen, or attempted to sway the top recruits at their official visits. Each recruiter tried to outwork and outsmart the others to bring home the four-star and five-star recruits that could mean a championship team instead of a runner-up finish.

In a more subtle way, but just as intently and for a much longer period of time, God spends a lifetime recruiting us to join his team. Just like football teams, God replenishes his eternal team each year with new recruits. Just like the coaches who are passionate about their teams and universities, God needs Christians who will recruit for Jesus because they are passionate about God and will share their faith stories. Hear this. Unlike recruiters who line up players that come and go, God never stops working to woo us to his team permanently. God works hard at it because since Adam and Eve suffered the fall from grace in the garden, every boy and girl is born a sinner. We don't become Christians by birthright, or good deeds, or living in a Christian home. Everyone eventually selects a team for eternity. Satan's team looks like a lot of fun in the beginning because there is pleasure in sin. If sin weren't fun, people wouldn't succumb to it. As a young man in my Sunday school class observed, Satan doesn't appear as a red-tailed devil with a pitchfork, but he lurks in familiar scenes around every corner. Satan's team brings us only heartache and bitter pain in the end.

God is longsuffering and wants to see every person come to know Jesus Christ. God woos us and longs for us to join his team, and he creates a unique plan for each of his five-star recruits. Believe it or not, you are a five-star recruit in God's eyes. Coaches have their eyes on five-star football recruits from the time they enter eighth grade. God loves you perfectly and had his eyes on you even before you were born.

Despite any past failings, iniquities, and current strongholds, you're still a hotshot recruit. God thinks you are uniquely the greatest thing to come along because he fearfully and wonderfully made you with special talents and a passion for those talents. So you don't believe all the recruiting hype and promises from the football recruiters? You can believe the promises that God makes and stand on them. You can know full well that whatever he has promised, you will receive because God is a promise keeper.

Prayer: Most Holy Lord God Almighty, it's exciting to know that you see me as a five-star recruit despite the many times that I have failed you and will fail you still. You are so good to me and want to enrich my life and save me if I will only put my trust in Jesus. Help me live up to my end of the recruiting deal. In Jesus's name, amen.

FB48:
AM I WILLING TO BE RUDY?

PHILIPPIANS 2:17, 4:12

I've learned by now to be quite content, whatever my
circumstances...

—Philippians 4:12 (MSG)

Rudy is one of my favorite sports movies. The movie is about
Rudy Ruettiger, a walk-on at Notre Dame. Rudy is pint-sized
and athletically challenged compared to the scholarship football
players at Notre Dame, but he has a heart the size of a mountain.
He would do anything that he possibly can to run through the
tunnel at Notre Dame Stadium just one time. But first, he must
get into Notre Dame because his academics didn't qualify him.

After he overcomes that monumental hurdle by the skin of
his teeth, a minor miracle in itself, he makes the scout team by
beating out a dozen other boys for one position. His job on the
scout team is to mimic the opposition's defense against the first-
team's offense. Rudy gets pulverized, battered, and bruised week
after week. Each Friday, he looks for his name on the dress-out
list, and it is never there until the last Friday, after all of his teammates insist to the head coach that he dress in his final game as a
senior. Rudy not only gets the thrill of dressing out and running
through the tunnel, but he gets into the game and makes a sack
on the final play of his career.

It's a sappy, tear-jerking storybook ending for a young man who never quit and never gave up. Rudy's ultimate reward of running out of the tunnel was eclipsed by the tackle that got him into the Notre Dame record book. Perhaps Rudy never even imagined playing; he simply wanted to dress so that his father would know that he was on the team.

Indianapolis and New Orleans competed for the 2010 Super Bowl trophy, which was won by New Orleans. The Colts and Saints were led by two outstanding quarterbacks, Peyton Manning and Drew Brees. The problem is that most of us want to be like Peyton and Drew, and we don't want to be Rudy. Peyton and Drew are much more exciting, and Rudy? Well, he's just got too much to overcome, and he will never get the headlines. But God has a plan for each of our lives, and that plan (I am sorry to break this to you) might not call for you to be the Peyton Manning or Drew Brees of your school, your office, your church, or even your family. What the plan calls for is to love God and to be obedient. If you will be faithful and stick it out like Rudy did, your just rewards will come.

There are many different positions to be played on God's team. Some positions are more prestigious than others. Your position might be one of the least attractive. You might just be a tremendous encourager so that when the stars with the big assignments feel down, you share just the right words to lift them up and refocus them on God's work. As believers, we can take a page out of Rudy's work ethic and commit to work day in and day out for God wherever he needs us. No matter how obscure the circumstances, God can and will do great and mighty things through us and for us.

> Prayer: Father God, may we learn from the wonderful story of perseverance in this classic movie. Even if I don't get any credit, may I be bursting with joy just from the opportunity to be on your team. When I am obedient, I know that you will give me playing time. May I never grow

tired of serving your kingdom. When I stumble and fall and life has me looking out of the ear hole of my helmet, I know that you will pull me out of the mire, straighten my helmet, pat me on my shoulder pads, and get me back into the game of life. In Jesus's name, amen.

FB49:
WINNING WAS A BREES

2 CORINTHIANS 12:6, JAMES 2:17

I don't want anyone to think more highly of me than he should, than what he can actually see in my life and my message.

—2 Corinthians 12:6 (TLB)

I watched the 2010 Super Bowl along with a record 106 million viewers. The game featured two of America's favorite athletes: Drew Brees of the New Orleans Saints and Peyton Manning of the Indianapolis Colts. The 31–17 victory meant so very much to the city of New Orleans to have their first world championship in forty-four years of professional sports. How fitting that the Saints parade came during Mardi Gras. The irony was that the man who stood in the way was once a huge Saints fan because his dad played for the Saints. A native of New Orleans, as a child, Peyton Manning and his older brother, Cooper, and younger brother, Eli, spent many Sunday afternoons in the Superdome, watching the Saints lose as Archie would get pummeled by one more defense. As the Saints fans booed Archie one day, Cooper, who was seven, asked his mother, Olivia, "Can we boo too, Mom?"

Super Bowl XLIV had great story lines and was extremely well played with very few penalties. One story line that many people would not recognize is that both starting quarterbacks are believers. In the book *Manning* by John Underwood, Peyton recalled the encounter with God that led him to proclaim Jesus Christ as his Savior. Thirteen-year-old Peyton heard the oft-repeated question from the pulpit of his church in New Orleans one Sunday morning: "If you died today, are you one hundred percent sure that you are going to heaven?" The message spoke to Peyton differently than it did to his brothers, and he felt small in the big church. When the pastor asked who wanted the assurance of eternity in heaven, Peyton raised his hand. He found the courage to come forward and take a stand that day for Jesus Christ. Peyton shared that while he has no problem with players taking more overt stands for Christ, he prefers to let his actions speak. He is aware that Christians make mistakes just like those who do not know Christ and that he is forgiven through Jesus Christ. In my opinion, Peyton has done a marvelous job being a role model in a high-profile, pressure-filled sport. He displayed grace and humility as he answered postgame questions from the Super Bowl media who were making way too much of one ill-advised throw.

The lesser-known quarterback was Drew Brees, who was on the cover of FCA's January/February 2010 *Sharing the Victory* magazine. Brees described the encounter that led him to Christ. When he was seventeen, his Austin, Texas, pastor asked the congregation if there were any who were willing to be one of a "few good men" for Jesus Christ. Drew made his commitment to Jesus Christ that morning. Soon, his high school football career blossomed, and he led Purdue to the Rose Bowl and starred for the San Diego Chargers. But an injury made him a backup, and he was traded to New Orleans in 2005. He came to a team with a tradition of mediocrity and no home games in a city ravaged by Hurricane Katrina. Drew was disconsolate about the trade, his new home, and his career. When he moved to New Orleans, he was immediately befriended by Cooper Manning, Peyton's brother. Drew recovered from his injury and thrived under Coach

Sean Payton. He made good on his "few good men" commitment and became a leader on the field, in the locker room, and, most importantly, in the community. Drew and his wife Brittany have helped raise over six million dollars through the Brees Dream Foundation to help the children of New Orleans, San Diego, and West Lafayette, Indiana.

These were two talented quarterbacks who desperately wanted to achieve the pinnacle of their profession. One celebrated the victory, and the other contemplated what might have been. But both understand that greater things await them in God's kingdom now and forever. Through the sacrifice made by God's own Son, may God be glorified in our stadiums and arenas.

> Prayer: Father God, thank you for the incredible theatre of sports that reveals character. May you receive all the glory when your children lead their teams and honor you with their efforts. May someone see Jesus Christ in me today. In Jesus's holy and precious name, amen.

FB50:
IF I WERE A BETTING MAN

JOHN 3:16-17

God did not send His Son into the world to condemn it, but to save it.

—John 3:17 (TLB)

One of our high school students in Sunday school shared that his friend's dad placed a $4,000 bet on the Saints–Colts Super Bowl game. Across the country, billions of dollars were placed on Super Bowl XLIV in office pools and through bookies in Vegas. The big winners were the bookies, who cleared hundreds of millions of dollars from this game by controlling the betting line. Their goal was to get as much money on the game as possible by shifting the point spread to balance the betting on the two teams and simply take their 10 percent. You could even bet on the first player to score a touchdown, the number of points scored in the game (called the over-under), and any number of statistical aspects of the game. After the game, people brag about their betting wins at the water cooler, and the ones who lost keep it to themselves.

Disclaimer: I do not condone betting, which can become an idol in a person's life and an addiction, just as alcoholism and drugs can.

After I became a Christian, I had no desire to wager on sporting events or even friendly golf matches. But I remember my first parlay card in college. What a thrill it was to win $25 on a five-dollar bet. I picked three underdogs to beat the spread as I proved my superior football knowledge. Of course, there are the times that I didn't win that I don't talk about. If only our study of the Bible was as intense as the analysis of Indianapolis defensive end Dwight Freeney's sprained right ankle prior to the 2010 Super Bowl.

Many people will bet big sums in hopes of a quick payoff to balance previous losses or to offset the impact of our struggling economy. Many of the same people are betting their lives last at least one more day before they receive Jesus Christ into their lives. There will come a day for each person that God will call your bluff and ask you to place all of your cards on the table. That day is known as judgment day, and God will be seated on the Great White Throne. If you know Jesus, he will speak for you. If you don't know Jesus, you will be the one answering to God. You will get to explain why you squandered your life on temporary pleasures and selfish pursuits. Each morning, millions of people bet they are going to leave and return home safely in cars, trains, and planes. It's a risk to walk out that door without Jesus Christ. Why would a person ever bet against Christ if they believe there is a God and that our God is a God of justice? One reason is a false sense of security that comes from a hardened heart.

I shudder when I think about how I bet the farm on some risky situations as an unsaved teenager. When I was fifteen, I sat in the backseat of a souped-up Chevy SS 396 as David pushed the speedometer needle to the H going back to school from PE. That was the H as in MPH, which was to the left of 120 at the bottom of the odometer. Was I so insecure and needed attention that badly in order to brag about how fast the car I was riding in was going? There was the night that six of us sped down a dirt road at 100 mph as the car floated like a magic carpet. If either car had wrecked, I would have been history forever where it's jalapeno hot.

As adults, the odds of dying increase each year. But it doesn't shake some of us that we need Christ until we hear the dreaded C-word, or until we hit rock bottom with addictions, or until we finally hear the gospel presented in a way that shakes our foundations.

You certainly have nothing to lose if you bet that there is a God. If somehow there wasn't a God, you haven't lost anything. But if you bet there isn't a God and there is, you've lost everything. Of course, there is a God, and when you put your faith in him, you've gained everything for eternity in heaven. What will it be?

As the same Sunday school class concluded with prayer requests, one student shared that her math teacher had been brutally murdered only three days before. The teacher was at school on Thursday and gone on Friday; here today, gone tomorrow. Only God knows where that teacher had placed his faith. With whom does your eternal life assurance policy lie? I pray that your policy is based solely on the death and resurrection of Jesus Christ. If it isn't, today is the best day to take out a policy in the Lord that will beat all odds.

> Prayer: Dear most gracious and wonderful Father God, thank you for the eternal life assurance policy that I have received when I turned from my sinful life and placed my faith in Jesus Christ. I am so thankful that you redeemed me and that I don't roll the dice for eternity every time I get in a car or a plane. I am at peace because I know my final destination. In the holy name of Jesus and his saving grace, amen.

FB51:
OVERCOMING ADVERSITY

PSALM 18:29, JOHN 16:33

In this world you will have tribulation, but be of good cheer, for I have overcome the world.

—John 16:33

It was the final game that I would attend as a student at the University of Georgia as we played our archrival Georgia Tech. Anticipation was high because Georgia had enjoyed a surprisingly good season. The temperature was unseasonably warm for the Saturday after Thanksgiving, in the seventies, and it was a perfect day for college football in Athens before a sellout crowd of sixty thousand fans.

The game started terribly for the Dawgs due to three early turnovers in Georgia territory, and Georgia trailed 20–0 late in the first quarter. But the Dawgs rallied with a couple of touchdowns, and Scott Woerner took a punt sixty-five yards for a touchdown to give the Dawgs a 21–20 lead late in the second half. However, speedster Drew Hill from Georgia Tech took the ensuing kickoff a hundred yards for a touchdown, and the air just seemed to come out of Sanford Stadium as the Tech contingent cheered deliriously in the northwest corner.

On Georgia's final drive with two minutes remaining, freshman Buck Belue rolled right on fourth and two and searched desperately for an open receiver. Amazingly, Amp Arnold had broken clear of the Tech secondary and Buck hit him for a long touchdown. Coach Vince Dooley made the decision to go for two in an attempt to win the game. Buck rolled left and was tackled. Just before his knees hit the turf, he pitched the ball to Arnold, who easily scampered into the end zone for two points, giving the Dawgs a thrilling 29–28 win. The chapel bell on North Campus tolled throughout the night in celebration of the hard-fought win.

Georgia overcame numerous adversities during the game to achieve the victory. Throughout our lives, we will be faced with numerous obstacles, and we can also be triumphant. Psalm 18:29 assures that we can leap over walls because we have the strength of the Lord. We are also assured that Christ has overcome the world, and that God will never leave us nor forsake us. Sometimes, the consequences of our actions will result in obstacles, and other times, God will put up walls simply to test our faith. No matter the trials we face, we can always be assured that God is in us, for us, and with us to help us be victorious.

> Prayer: Father God, thank you for the assurance that I have through Jesus Christ, who overcame the greatest of all adversities when he beat death by rising from the grave. For that reason and through your promises in the Bible, I can cling to the hope that is available to me and to every person who confesses you as Savior and Lord. In the holy and wonderful name of Jesus Christ, amen.

FB52:
CRUNCH TIME

PSALM 119:100-105

I understand more than the ancients, because I keep your precepts.

—Psalm 119:100

NFL and major college football teams have a playbook that is about three inches thick with hundreds of offensive plays. These plays are studied by each player and rehearsed again and again. The pressure is especially on the quarterbacks because as the decision makers, they must know the second and third options in case the first option breaks down. When the pressure is on and the quarterback calls "Z-87 trap swing right overload," each player must know where to run and who to block for the play to work. If the players don't know the plays, it's pretty obvious that the chance to win the game will be slim to none.

There comes a time for all of us when we're faced with pressure-packed situations and dire circumstances. It could be personal illness, the death of loved ones, betrayal by close friends, or job loss. These events can leave us reeling and fill us with the FUD factor: fear, uncertainty, and doubt.

The Bible gives us instruction for everything that Satan and life can throw at us. We must know now that the Word of God is Truth and that the Truth will sustain us when nothing else will.

Just like the playbook, the Bible has guidance for any situation that life brings us.

But we can't just open the Bible when we're in dire straits or in the middle of a hotly contested battle with Satan. We must be constantly studying the Bible when things are going well in order to know where to go for the perfect Scripture that will sustain us through tough times. Setbacks in life can take us where we've never been, and we won't know how to respond in faith without the knowledge and instruction from the inspired Word of the living Almighty Creator.

We need to understand it, memorize it, and be able to regurgitate it to sustain ourselves and our loved ones. The Bible is full of promises, but we need to know the promises to be able to stand on them. What are some of the most important promises in the Bible? That Christ died once for all of our sins (John 3:16–17), that God will never leave us nor forsake us (Hebrews 13:5), and that the Holy Spirit will help us with our daily problems (Romans 8:26). There is always hope through Christ Jesus, who experienced all of the pitfalls and emotions that we will ever encounter. With God, we will never walk alone, and Jesus has already walked where we're walking, no matter how dark the path (Psalm 119:105).

> Prayer: Father God, help me constantly turn to the Bible and understand your magnificent promises that are available to me even though I am a sinner. Thank you for your forgiveness and the grace through Jesus Christ, which I cannot earn. In the holy name of our precious Lord and Savior, amen.

FB53:
I'M GOING TO DISNEY WORLD!

PHILIPPIANS 1:6

He who has begun a good work in you will complete it…

Usually, it takes six to eight years to make a complete quarter-back in the NFL. Rookie quarterbacks come into the NFL with the ability to throw the ball hard and throw it a long way. But in the first few years come the inevitable interceptions. What signal caller threw twenty-four interceptions and only six touchdown passes in his first NFL year? It was none other than four-time Super Bowl champion Terry Bradshaw.

There are so many challenges that young quarterbacks must overcome. A young quarterback must learn to put touch on the ball in order to loft it over dropping linebackers. The NFL cornerbacks are so much quicker and more physical than the college corners, and they don't drop balls thrown near them. Consider the vast experience and knowledge that are needed by the NFL quarterbacks to read complex defenses, which are much more complicated than the defenses in the college game. The quarterback must also learn to manage the clock in the last two minutes of the game. Finally, there is the ability to perform in the Super Bowl, the most intense, pressure-packed game that is watched by over 100 million Americans. When all of these facets of the game are mastered, the maturation of the quarterback is complete. As he waves the Super Bowl trophy after conquering that pressure, it's no small wonder he yells, "I'm going to Disney World!"

It takes God an entire lifetime to complete us, and it is never complete until we win our faith "Super Bowl" and leave this earth to be with God in heaven. We mature by diligently studying his word, by frequent and fervent prayer, and by learning to apply our faith to all facets of our lives. We must learn to trust in God and have faith in him during our toughest times. God uses these situations to sanctify us or make us more holy.

> Prayer: Father God, just like tough times make NFL quarterbacks better so that they can reach the pinnacle of their game, help me reach your pinnacle. Give me a hunger and a thirst and a desire to be as holy as possible and to give you the glory. Forgive me when I fail to be obedient. In the name of Jesus, amen.

FB54:
TOUCHDOWN MOSES!

EXODUS 17:11-14

Aaron and Hur stayed up his hands, the one on the one side, and the other on the other side; and his hands were steady until the going down of the sun.

—Exodus 17:12

It is widely known that the six-story-tall mural of Jesus at the University of Notre Dame in South Bend, Indiana, is known as "Touchdown Jesus." In the mural, Jesus has both arms in the air, and it does look like he is signaling touchdown just as a linesman would. The dramatic mural was captured on film in the movie *Rudy*. Surely it is an awe-inspiring scene for the Notre Dame students and faculty to be able to see daily. Touchdown Jesus certainly beats the larger-than-life pictures of athletes that Nike plasters on downtown buildings in Manhattan and Los Angeles.

Moses heeded God's call to lead the Israelites, God's chosen people, out of Egypt, where the Pharaohs had kept them in bondage for four hundred years. After they escaped Egypt for the promised land, Israel would battle different sects of people for rule over the land.

One day, God's chosen people fought the Amalekites. Moses might have been the first person in the Bible to signal touchdown. Israel was winning so long as Moses held his arms in the air. But when he dropped his arms, Big Mo (Momentum, not Moses) hopped on the Amalekites' bench. Moses held his arms in the air for a long time, and he got very tired. So he called in his brother Aaron and a man named Hur to prop up his arms. The reason is that as long as Moses diligently held up his arms, God gave Israel the power to "score the winning touchdown" and defeat the Amalekites.

> Prayer: Father God, thank you for the legacy of Moses and for all of your prophets who spoke your truth. In Jesus's name, amen.

Note: An interesting sidebar is that there is no remnant of the people known as Amalekites. God was true to his promise that they would be removed from the face of the earth (Exodus 17).

FB55:
BREAKING TACKLES

HEBREWS 12:1

Therefore, since we are surrounded by such a great cloud of witnesses, let us throw off everything that hinders and the sin that so easily entangles us. And let us run with perseverance the race marked out for us. (NIV)

The goal of any running back is to put the football over the goal line for six points. There have been some great touchdown runs in football history. The greatest run that I ever saw was by a quarterback, Steve Young, who broke eight tackles on the way to a forty-yard touchdown. The game was played in San Francisco, and it was third down and long when he began his scramble. Young swiveled his hips and shed tackler after tackler. Nothing or nobody was going to slow him down, and he collapsed from exhaustion after crossing the goal line for the touchdown.

In 1959, Billy Cannon's eighty-nine-yard punt return on Halloween night in fog-shrouded Tiger Stadium gave LSU a 7–3 win over Ole Miss that sealed the national championship. Cannon was "Cannon-ized" as the Heisman Trophy winner and the most famous football player in LSU lore. He fielded the punt near the LSU ten and, through clever moves and tremendous balance, shed arm tackle after arm tackle by the Ole Miss defenders. He finally broke clear of the pack at the Ole Miss thirty. What's amusing in the grainy YouTube video is that the official running with him is actually running faster than a very tired Cannon as he crosses the goal line.

The author of Hebrews challenges us to be just as determined to obey God in our daily lives as the great runners in football strive to keep from being tackled. Satan tries to tackle us each day, trip us up from serving the kingdom, and interrupt our obedience to God. If Satan can make us disobedient, he can stop our work for the kingdom. When we are apart from God due to the entanglement of sin in our lives, it's a sure thing that nobody will get saved during our self-centered actions.

When we confess our sins and receive God's forgiveness, God removes the tangles that keep us from scoring touchdowns for the kingdom. God always gives us a way to break through any obstacle that Satan uses to bring us down short of his goal line.

> Prayer: Father God, thank you for giving me ways to avoid the entanglement of sin that threatens to bring me down and make me ineffective. You are so good to me all the time, Lord. Thank you. In Jesus's name, amen.

FB56:
GAMEDAY OUTLOOK

GALATIANS 5:22-23

But the fruit of the Spirit is love, joy, peace, patience, kindness, goodness, gentleness, faithfulness, and self-control…

When a big college or pro football game occurs, the experts will compare the different facets of the teams and determine which is the stronger in each area. The team with the stronger component is given the X. The team with the most Xs, Texas, will be favored to win this game.

Texas-Nebraska Comparison		
Area	Texas	Nebraska
Quarterback	X	
Running Back	X	
Offensive Line		X
Receivers	X	
Kicking Game		X
Defensive Line	X	
Linebackers	X	
Defensive Backs		X
Intangibles	X	
Coaching	X	

Fruit of the Spirit Comparison		
	Believer	Unbeliever
Love	X	
Joy	X	
Peace	X	
Patience	X	
Kindness	X	
Goodness	X	
Faithfulness	X	
Gentleness	X	
Self-Control	X	

When you compare a believer who is solid in Christ in all phases of his or her life to an unbeliever who does not have the Holy Spirit, the comparison is one-sided. It's no contest. The believer who is strong in obedience to Christ will ache for those who are unsaved, find joy in difficult circumstances, and consistently have more peace. The believer should usually have more patience, and kindness and goodness will be demonstrated through good deeds in the name of Jesus Christ. The believer should walk by faith, be gentle to his fellow man, and control his anger. A tall order? Certainly. Infallible? Certainly not. But anything is possible with God. Is the believer better than the unbeliever? Certainly not. But the believer has one distinct advantage. The believer has been washed in the saving blood of Christ and received the seal of the Comforter, the Holy Spirit. Advantage: believer.

> Prayer: Father God, may I understand that I do have an advantage over those who are unsaved. Help me be pure so that I can consistently exhibit the fruit of the Spirit and bring honor, glory, and praise to your holy name. In the wonderful name of Jesus Christ, who is our precious Lord and Savior, amen.

FB57:
THE SIZE OF THE FIGHT
IN THE DOG

2 CORINTHIANS 4:18

We look not at what can be seen but at what cannot be
seen; for what can be seen is temporary but what cannot
be seen is eternal. (TLB)

When a college team like the University of Georgia signs a
recruiting class, fans enjoy reading the statistics and swooning
over the size of the players. Fans get excited when the team has
signed a behemoth six-foot six-inch, 325-pound offensive lineman or a six-foot, 215-pound running back with blazing 4.4
speed. The players look very impressive at first sight and on paper,
but sadly, some of them will never play a down due to injury, bad
grades, or simply not having a strong enough will to compete
at the D-I level. Despite the predictions of the experts, there is
really no way to predict how each player will fare.

An old saying is what really counts is not the size of the dog
in the fight but the size of the fight in the dog. You can see how
big the dog is, but you can't tell what's in the dog's heart. The best
coaches are able to identify how to get the most desire out of
these players during the next four years.

"We look not at what can be seen, but at what cannot be seen. For what can be seen is temporary, but what cannot be seen is eternal" (2 Corinthians 4:18). The awesome speed and strength of each player is fleeting and temporary. As his speed decreases and strength is diminished, a player will eventually be replaced by a faster, younger, and stronger player. When the player is no longer able to compete and must retire, how will the player adjust to his new life after football?

If the player's faith in Jesus Christ is strong, he will have a much better chance of dealing with retirement from competition. If the player's heart is grounded in Christ, he knows that eternal awards await that are so much greater than the fleeting fame and fortune that he once experienced. A player who knows Jesus Christ personally will be able to find joy more often despite circumstances and become more productive for the kingdom.

> Prayer: Father God, may I display a portion of the heart that you displayed when you fought for your life on the cross. Thank you for loving me so much that you would stay on the cross for me. In Jesus's name, amen.

FB58:
TAKE ONE FOR HIS TEAM

JOHN 18:3-11

Jesus answered, "I have told you that I am He: if therefore you seek Me, let these go their way."

—John 18:8 (KJV)

An admirable character trait displayed by a coach is when he is willing to give credit to his team for a win and take the blame for a loss. In this day of online blogs, Twitter, websites, and online newspapers all vying for attention, the writers and bloggers and radio hosts come looking for blood when the team loses. But the admirable coach will step up to the microphone and say, "I know you want to know what happened. The players played their hearts out. I didn't prepare us well enough. I didn't anticipate the defense they would use in the second half. I made a decision on fourth and three that I wish I had back. I should have kicked the field goal when we were down nine. It was my fault, and it's my responsibility to have us better prepared." That coach essentially said, "Leave them [my players] alone. It's me you want." Even though he might have been fearful that admitting fault could cost him his job, those players will play even harder for him the next game.

Jesus took one for his team in the garden of Gethsemane. When Judas brought the Roman soldiers to arrest him with their weapons and torches, they were looking for blood. Jesus protected his disciples by asking, "Who is it you seek?" He asked the soldiers twice and said, "Take me." Jesus protected his disciples even though he knew they would flee at the first sign of danger.

There is no doubt that the disciples deeply appreciated the love that their Savior showed them when they didn't deserve it. Once they received the baptism of the Holy Spirit, they played their hearts out for Christ and changed this world forever.

Prayer: Father God, help me play my heart out for you this day. I could never repay you sufficiently. In Jesus's name, amen.

FB59:
YOUR DADDY MUST BE CRAZY!

JOHN 3:16-17

For God did not send His Son into the world to condemn
it, but to save it.

—John 3:17 (TLB)

This story was shared with me and our high school boys at open
gym one evening by my brother in Christ, Paul Sligar. In the
1980s, two Class A teams in Mississippi vied for the final play-
off spot to advance to the state playoffs. Tishimingo led by two
points, 16–14, late in the fourth quarter and had the ball on the
opponents' forty-yard line. There was not enough time left for a
touchdown drive. The Tishimingo coach called his son, the quarterback, over to the sideline and said, "Son, I know this sounds
crazy, but I need you to give the ball to our tailback. Tell him to
run sixty yards in the wrong direction."

The QB said, "Dad, are you kidding?"

The coach replied, "Son, just trust me."

The QB relayed the play in the huddle, and the team drew
a delay of game penalty because of the confusion. When the
QB called the play again, the tailback said, "Your daddy must
be crazy!"

But Tishimingo executed the play, and the tailback ran through
the back of Tishimingo's end zone for a safety, which tied the

game at 16–16. The game went into overtime, and Tishimingo scored a touchdown to win the game 22–16.

It turned out that the head coach had information none of his players had. He knew that his team needed to win the game by four points or more to advance to the state playoffs. Eventually, they placed their trust in his seemingly wacky advice and won the game. God also has information that none of us have. He knows that we must commit our lives to Christ if we are to experience eternal life now and forever with him in heaven. It sounds wacky to give your life to a man who died on a cross two thousand years ago. But God knows how the game ends, and we must trust his advice. Place your trust in Christ and advance to the eternal playoffs in heaven.

> Prayer: Father God, before I was a believer, I thought that the story was a crazy one. But I know it's real, and I can't wait to see how the story ends when I get to see Jesus face to face. In the precious name of my Savior and Lord, amen.

FB60:
RUNNING FIRST STRING
OR THIRD STRING?

JEREMIAH 17:5-8, 29:11; JOHN 21:19

Follow me.

—John 21:19

A football team builds its offense around key players such as a triple-threat quarterback. If the first-string QB runs a 4.4 forty-yard dash and has the arm to gun the ball sixty-five yards in the air, the offensive coordinator will use the full repertoire of plays to take advantage of his skills. However, this player is very difficult to replace when he is injured. If the second-string quarterback is also injured and the third-string quarterback has 5.2 speed and can only make the short and medium throws, the coordinator must reduce his play calling to a few basic plays. This severe limitation enables the defense to put eight in the box and play the run much more aggressively, making it very difficult for the offense to score enough points to win the game. We need to use our entire repertoire of kingdom plays to overcome the defense of the enemy.

In his book *This Day with the Master*, Reverend Dennis Kinlaw points out that when we fail to surrender our lives completely to

Christ, we force God to shrink the game plan that he has for our lives. God has key plays that he wants us to run, but if sins such as pride, selfishness, worry, and disobedience separate us from him, many kingdom plays must go back on his shelf. When we fail to develop our spiritual lives to the fullest extent, we limit his play calling from those suited for a first stringer to a third stringer.

God is much more concerned about our *availability* than our ability because it is God who empowers us to do things that we never dreamed we were capable of doing. We are all capable of sharing the gospel effectively through his unique plans for us and circumstances that he arranges in our lives.

What is the key to executing God's complete game plan? Jesus put it very simply. He said, "Follow me." Follow Jesus. God alone gives us the strength and power to execute his game plans, but we must do it through him. He must always be part of our plans. Apart from God, we can do nothing (John 15:5).

Prayer: Most holy, gracious, and merciful God, may I realize what an awesome contribution that I could be making to your kingdom. I want to commit myself to your plan for me, not my plan for me. I want to stand before you one day and know that you received my best. In Jesus's holy name, amen.

FB61:
JOE WILLIE'S SCARS

JOHN 20:25-29, 2 CORINTHIANS 5:7

Unless I see in his hands the print of the nails… I will not believe.

—John 20:25

Joe Willie Namath was one of the most popular players in football during the 1960s and 1970s. "Broadway Joe" was an All-American quarterback at Alabama and suffered his first knee injury during his senior season. Namath played for the New York Jets of the upstart American Football League. The AFL was the little brother to the established NFL until Joe led the New York Jets to a 16–7 upset victory over the Baltimore Colts in Super Bowl III. Even though the Jets were seventeen-point underdogs, Joe brashly guaranteed a win at a poolside interview three days before the game. The incredible upset helped position the AFL as the equal to the NFL, and the AFL merged with the NFL two years later. The NFL teams were divided into the American Conference and the National Conference, which is how they are still divided.

After his stunning Super Bowl victory, Joe played nine more seasons and had four serious knee operations. Eventually, Joe would have both knees replaced long after his playing days were over.

Let's fast forward over twenty-five years after Super Bowl III to a steamy, hot summer night at Disney's Epcot. Becca, Allison, Jillian, and I had just spent a long day at Disney World. After the fireworks show, we boarded a small boat that stops at the various onsite Disney resorts. Nobody was talking. I think everybody was just drained from the heat. At the next stop, a man and his two young daughters boarded. The man and the girls took the seat directly behind us. *There is something vaguely familiar about his silhouette,* I thought. *He might be Broadway Joe! I can know for sure if I get a good look at his knees.* Very slowly, I leaned forward and peeked over my left shoulder. There was the proof: a foot-long, zipper-like scar on the inside of each knee. *I know it's him!* I didn't speak because if the people on the boat knew, he would have been swamped with autograph requests.

Joe and his daughters departed at the very next stop. As they walked toward their resort hotel, I turned to Becca and said in a medium voice, "Becca, you know who that was? Joe Namath."

Immediately, the boat came to life. A woman behind me said, "Joe Namath? Really? I can't believe he was on this boat."

A second woman gushed, "I *loved* Joe Namath."

No one questioned me that I had made up the story. They took my word for it. After all, I had seen the scars.

Let's consider the reactions of the disciples when Mary Magdalene and the other Mary breathlessly shared their eyewitness accounts that the tomb was empty and Jesus had risen. The disciples didn't believe the women. They finally believed when Jesus appeared to them in the upper room.

All of them believed except Thomas. Thomas said he would believe only if he saw the scars and felt them. When Thomas saw the nail-scarred hands of Jesus eight days later, he exclaimed, "My Lord and my God!"

Jesus replied, "Because you have seen Me, you believe. Those who do not see Me and believe are blessed" (John 20:28–29).

Are you blessed? We cannot see his scars that saved us from the grave, but as believers we walk by faith, not by sight (2 Corinthians 5:7).

On that Disney World boat I sat smugly, knowing that I had seen what no one else did. But I was blissfully ignorant that many people on the boat knew what I did not know: that Jesus had taken the nails for each of us. It would be almost ten more years before I came to the heart knowledge of this most important discovery.

> Prayer: Father God, thank you for the faith that enables me to believe even when I cannot see. Help me walk by faith, not by sight. I thank you for the scars that saved me for eternity when I finally believed. In Jesus's name, amen.

FB62:
IN SEASON AND OUT

2 TIMOTHY 4:2

Preach the Word of God urgently at all times, whenever you get the chance, in season and out, when it is convenient and when it is not.

Many people believe that the state of Alabama has the most passionate college football fan base in America. There are several reasons, including proud winning traditions at the two major universities, which frankly dislike each other's program, and an absence of professional teams. It has long been said that there are two sports seasons in Alabama, football during football season, and football recruiting when the football season is over.

It appears that in the decade beginning with the year 2000, there are two sports seasons in the SEC—football and football recruiting—that last 24/7, 365 days a year. At one time, there was a signing day in February for seniors, and this day was preceded by five or six weekends of college visits. Then juniors began announcing early verbal commitments at various times during the year. Because these announcements can happen at any time the way the current rules stand, you can have football recruiting news on any given day of the year.

Just as football and football recruiting extend the football year to all 365 days, Paul taught us in 2 Timothy that Christians should follow a 24/7 365-days-a-year schedule for sharing the gospel. He declared that there are two times for preaching the gospel urgently. Those times are when we are moved by the Holy Spirit, and on those days when we have the blahs and can't believe our efforts would be fruitful. We are placing way too much importance on ourselves when we believe that we need to be perfect in telling people about Christ. God will use the most feeble and botched attempts to draw people to his Son, Jesus Christ. Looking for opportunities to share the gospel and God's love should be on our minds each day when we leave the house and begin to interact with the public.

> Prayer: Father God, help me realize that there are opportunities to share what you have done in my life at times other than Christmas and Easter. May I be obedient and have my eyes to see and ears to hear where you are at work and join you there. In Jesus's name, amen.

FB63:
OUR TWELFTH MAN

PSALM 46:1, DANIEL 3:12-25

Then Nebuchadnezzar the king was astonished, and rose up in haste, and spake, and said unto his counsellors, "Did not we cast three men bound into the midst of the fire?" They answered and said unto the king, "True, O king." He answered and said, "Lo, I see four men loose, walking in the midst of the fire, and they have no hurt; and the form of the fourth is like the Son of God."

—Daniel 3:24–25

Texas A&M University fans support their football team with great passion. Perhaps their passion is best exemplified by the tradition of the twelfth man. This tradition was once ranked number three of all college football traditions. Kyle Field earns its nickname, "The Home of the Twelfth Man," from this tradition of the team and the pride of many fans that stand throughout every game. When Coach Dana Bible was shorthanded in a game against Centre College in 1922, he asked former player E. King Gill to be his twelfth man in case his team needed him. Gill did not play in the game but stood on the sidelines throughout the game just in case. The Aggie fans never forgot the extra man who stood ready if needed.

The extra man on the Aggie sideline reminded me of Meshach, Shadrach, and Abednego, the three Hebrew lads in the book of Daniel. They told King Nebuchadnezzar that they believed that God would save them from harm and, furthermore, that they would never bow down to worship his golden idol. The furious king ordered the furnace to be heated seven times hotter than usual, a fire that was so hot that the men who heated the furnace died. The three lads were bound and cast into the furnace. Yet when the king and his court looked into the furnace, the boys were walking around, unharmed, with not one hair on their heads singed. Furthermore, they also had an extra man walking with them, a man who looked an awful lot like the Son of God. Many theological experts believe that the extra man was Jesus Christ.

When all was said and done, God proved to be stronger than Satan, as he always is. God stands by us and is our "ever present help in time of trouble" (Psalm 46:1). The Holy Spirit will be your extra man if you will allow it. How awesome it is that we can always turn to God when the odds are overwhelmingly against us.

> Prayer: Father God, thank you for your presence and for the presence of Jesus Christ, the extra man, in my life. Most of all, thank you for the sacrifice that Jesus made for me on the cross. I give you the honor, the glory, and the praise. In Jesus's name, amen.

FB64:
A STARTER'S ATTITUDE

PHILIPPIANS 2:17, 4:12

I've learned by now to be quite content, whatever my circumstances…

—Philippians 4:12 (MSG)

My friend Kevin told me about his experiences and attitude as a member of the scout team on his high school team in the Canadian province of Prince Edward Island. Kevin's story was very much like Rudy; he never got to play in the games but was dedicated to helping his team win on Friday night. As he described the practices, he said, "I was a starter four days a week," which I thought was a really cool attitude. True, he didn't get the accolades on Friday night as he stood on the sideline with the team, but he had the satisfaction that he had done everything he could to get his teammates ready for the game.

My dad played on the scout team at Hamilton (Alabama) High School in the 1920s. He was smaller than the other players, but he kept using his quickness to break up the offensive team's plays despite wearing makeshift football shoes with metal Coca-Cola bottle caps nailed to the soles for traction. Dad's high school coach, who played some college football, sent word that if Dad kept coming out for football, he "was going to get killed."

Yet Dad tried his hardest, although he too would never play a down of varsity football.

Wouldn't it be great to have the same attitude for Christ, doing whatever God puts in front of us without hesitation or complaints and doing it for his glory and not ours?

God has a plan for each of our lives, but that plan might not call for us to be the star players. The plan calls for us to love God and be obedient to him. If we will be faithful and stick it out, our just rewards will come in heaven. As believers, we can take a page out of these scout team experiences and commit to work day in and day out for God wherever he needs us. No matter how obscure the circumstances, God can and will do great and mighty things through us and for us.

> Prayer: Father God, even if I get no credit, may I burst with joy from the opportunity just to be on your team. Help me realize that my eternal reward is to join you in heaven. May I never grow tired of serving your kingdom. When I stumble and fall, please pull me back on my feet and get me back in the game of life. In Jesus's name, amen.

FB65:
HOT DIGGITY DOG!

LUKE 15:3-10

I say to you that likewise there will be more joy in heaven over one sinner who repents than over ninety-nine just persons who need no repentance.

—Luke 15:7

Once, I described how excited my daughter, Jillian, and her friend, Liz, were to find tickets for their first Georgia–Florida game in 2007. They were thrilled to find two tickets outside the stadium from two kindly UGA gentlemen who had extras. They were overjoyed just to get into Alltel Stadium.

However, I believe that their excitement was actually surpassed by the father from Alabama whose son surprised him with a ticket to the 2013 BCS Championship game that his son hid in his father's new hat. His son made the video that went viral within two days. Millions via YouTube, Twitter, and even ESPN saw the tears of joy streaming down his face.

I loved this story for many reasons. First, he showed great enthusiasm for his Christmas present, a new fedora, and shouted, "Hot diggity dog!" I haven't heard that saying in years. Second, he said that he wished he could have worn his new hat to church that morning. More brownie points for Dad that he had been to church.

After his son asked him what size the hat was, he looked inside the hat and saw the ticket with "BCS" on it. He wept as he held his good fortune in his hand and stared at it in sheer disbelief.

His unbridled glee reminded me of the saints in heaven who rejoice exceedingly over one lost sheep who is found (see Luke 15:4–7). If the collective joy of millions of angels and saints surpasses this gentleman's joy, I can't wait to get to heaven to become part of it!

Then the gentleman asked hopefully, "All of us?" As in are all of us going to the game? Certainly, he wanted his entire family to enjoy the experience. But his son replied, "No, pop, just you and me."

He and his son had their tickets in hand, so they were assured of going to Miami. But being a member of the family wouldn't get the other family members into the big game.

It's similar to getting into the big game that is played in heaven. Growing up in a Christian home, or hanging with your Christian friends, or having brothers or sisters who are believers will not gain you entrance to the big game. Only through personal repentance and the cleansing of the blood of the Lamb can anyone gain entrance to the ultimate BCS Game which is played in heaven. This opportunity is available to all and was made possible because Christ suffered on the cross.

> Prayer: Most gracious heavenly Father, thank you for the eternal gift of your resurrected Son, who paved the way for me to get into the big game. Renew my heart so that I react with the joy of the saints, and the next time I hear about a lost sheep coming into the fold, may I shout, "Hot diggity dog!" In the sweet name of Jesus, amen.

FB66:
MERCY FOR MALCOLM

NUMBERS 14:18, GALATIANS 5:22-23, HEBREWS 13:1-5

The Lord is longsuffering and abundant in mercy, forgiving iniquity and transgression.

—Numbers 14:18

On October 27, 2012, Georgia and Florida were locked in a heated battle midway through the fourth quarter in Jacksonville with Georgia clinging to a one-point lead, 10–9. Emotions were riding high on both sides throughout the game, and the officials had called numerous personal fouls for unsportsmanlike conduct. Georgia's Malcolm Mitchell caught a pass for a first down just across midfield, but he ran his mouth to a Florida cornerback after the play and received his second unsportsmanlike penalty of the second half.

As Becca and I watched the game from Okaloosa Island, Florida, I turned to her in disgust and said, "That's two personal fouls on Mitchell! Take him out and don't put him back in!"

On the Georgia sideline, you could see Head Coach Mark Richt giving Mitchell pointed feedback. Then, he placed his hand on Malcolm's shoulder pad and spoke to him very calmly, which must have been difficult to do in the heat of the moment.

On his postgame radio show, Coach Richt explained that he initially gave Malcolm the distinct impression that he might not play again in that game. But then Richt calmly explained that he would be held out of the game for one play, which gave Malcolm a chance to settle down.

On second down, Mitchell reentered the game and immediately caught a five-yard pass that was ruled complete after an extensive review by the replay official. On third and five, Aaron Murray connected with Mitchell on another short pass. Mitchell spun past the Florida cornerback and sped down the sideline. He cut to his right, split two defenders at the five, and raced into the end zone for the clinching touchdown!

I thought about my emotional outburst and how grateful I was that Coach Richt gave Mitchell another chance, because Mitchell came through with the biggest play of the season for the Bulldogs. Obviously, if I had been coach, he would never have received the opportunity. The episode caused me to think about how patient and merciful that God must be toward me. Numbers 14:18 says that "The Lord is longsuffering and abundant in mercy, forgiving iniquity and transgression." Goodness, how many opportunities could God have bailed on me because I kept making the same mistake over and over? Mistakes or sins such as worrying again and again instead of praying and trusting him. So many times he could have given up on me, but he never did and never will.

God's promise that we can always count on is that he will never leave us nor forsake us (Hebrews 13:5). In this very tense situation, Coach Richt chose not to forsake Mitchell. When he spoke calmly to him (and for that Georgia fans can be grateful), I felt that he exemplified the fruit of the Spirit, which is love, joy, peace, patience, kindness, goodness, gentleness, faithfulness, and self-control (Galatians 5:22–23).

Prayer: Most gracious and longsuffering God, thank you for the times too numerous to count when you have been so patient with me and so merciful to me. It's great to see examples in sports where a young person is given an extra chance and comes through and when one of your children bears fruit in the heat of the battle. I appreciate the unending love and faith that you have in me, even when my faith may be no bigger than a mustard seed. In Jesus's name, amen.

FB67: MEMORIES FOR A LIFETIME

PHILIPPIANS 3:13-14, 1 CORINTHIANS 9:24-27

Strain to reach the end of the race.

—Philippians 3:14 (TLB)

It was my privilege to serve as the team chaplain for the Roswell Hornets for the 2012 high school football season. I wasn't sure what I was committing to at first, but I quickly found out that being chaplain has a number of perks. I get to roam the sideline so I always have great views of plays, and I can offer encouragement to the players without the downside of correcting their mistakes.

The 2012 season had been one of disappointment and discouragement for the team, which was 2–7 going into the final Friday night of the season. Three tough losses by three points or less prevented the Hornets from enjoying a winning season and making the playoffs, and a six-game losing streak after an opening win had tried everyone's patience.

Roswell's final game was at home against powerful arch rival Walton, which was 7–2 and assured of the number two region seed. At halftime, the score was Walton 21, Roswell 7. Roswell lost its talented tailback, Andrew Kwetang, in the second quarter for the remainder of the game. The prospect of victory looked bleak as a pall hung over the Roswell locker room at halftime.

The locker room was again quiet after Coach Sanderson implored his players to dig deep inside and find anything possible to help turn the game around. As my dad would say, I was about to "bust a gut" to say something. After the coaches left the immediate locker room, I went over to the O-line, which was having trouble blocking the Walton defensive front. I told them forty years ago, my high school basketball career ended on a downer when I sprained my ankle, and that I still remembered that I left something on the floor that night. I told them that this (deficit) is not how you want to remember tonight. One player thanked me, and I left the locker room knowing that I had tried to encourage them.

Early in the third quarter, near midfield, Roswell senior QB Ryan Monty pitched the ball to Mechane Slade, the backup sophomore tailback. He broke through the line, juked two safeties on the fifteen, and went into the end zone! The score was 21–14, and the Roswell sideline came alive! Four plays later, Roswell senior linebacker Grant Beidel intercepted a pass and ran thirty yards for the tying score! After a Walton field goal, Monty hit senior Bennett Barton on a perfect pass down the left sideline for forty-five yards and the go-ahead touchdown, 28–24! Roswell made a tremendous defensive stand, then gained three first downs on the ground to run out the last four and a half minutes of the game for an astounding come-from-behind victory! As one man said, it's always good if you are Roswell when you beat one of the "tons," meaning Milton or Walton.

After the game, I am allowed to pray briefly with the team which gathers with the coaches and cheerleaders on the twenty-five yard line. I opened the prayer by thanking God for the memories of a lifetime. These young men had lost numerous close ball games in the past two years, but tonight, they closed the deal in the last game that many of them will ever play.

It was so heartwarming to watch the reactions of the seniors after the game. Several were very late leaving the field. Others came back out of the locker room to stare at the field, full uniforms still on. Two cried together, and one young man cried uncontrollably as I hugged him. The team had stayed together through a difficult season, continued to persevere and believe in themselves, and indeed found a way to play their best football of the season in the second half! The anguish and frustration of a tough season was wiped away with the healing salve of an unbelievable come-from-behind victory against a mighty foe.

The apostle Paul encouraged the new believers in Philippi to "strain to reach the end of the race and receive the prize" (Philippians 3:14, TLB). For the underdog Roswell seniors, their hope enabled them to strive to win the last game of their high school careers.

> Prayer: Most gracious Father, when the negativity of competitive sports threatens to overwhelm all that is good with sports, thank you for a special night when everything that happened seemed to glorify you. I thank you that ten, twenty, thirty, and even forty years later, Roswell's young men will fondly remember the magical comeback in the last game of their high school careers. In Jesus's name, amen.

FB68:
VICTORY IN CHRIST'S KINGDOM

JOHN 8:6-11

He that is without sin among you, let him first cast a stone.

—John 8:7

The troubled life of Philadelphia Eagles quarterback Michael Vick was well-chronicled. Vick perhaps fell further from grace than any athlete in his generation.

In 2006, the Atlanta Falcon quarterback was one of the most popular, talented football players in the NFL. When I spoke to Atlanta and Athens area FCA huddles during his heyday, I would ask the kids who their favorite athlete was. Vick was hands-down the most popular choice, and many kids considered him to be a role model.

In 2007, the stories broke of his horrific involvement in dog-fighting. Vick eventually served seventeen months in a maximum security prison in Leavenworth, Kansas, and six more months in a halfway house. Once the recipient of a $110 million contract, Vick owed between $10 to $15 million dollars after bad investments, foolish spending, and monstrous legal fees. Many people despised Vick. Others gave up on him and said he would never play football again.

Toward the end of Vick's Leavenworth term, Tony Dungy, the former Super Bowl coach and a well-known Christian, mentored Michael weekly and prayed with him. In 2009, the Philadelphia Eagles received criticism when they were the only NFL team to give him a second chance. Michael played sparingly, maintained a low profile, and stayed out of trouble.

In February 2010, with Tony Dungy standing by his side, Michael Vick shared his testimony at the annual Super Bowl breakfast that is sponsored by Athletes in Action and Campus Crusade for Christ. Art Stricklin of the *Baptist Press* captured these thoughts in a post-breakfast interview with Michael.

> "I feel I'm in the back seat now and God is in the front," Vick told *Baptist Press* in a post-breakfast interview. "Five months ago I was worried with what was going to happen (with the NFL), but now I'm more at peace. God has taken it over. I don't have to worry about being dynamic. God is in control of that."
>
> "I wanted a chance to redeem myself," he said. "Pre-incarceration it was all about me. When I got to prison, I realized I couldn't do it anymore. The one thing I could rely on was my faith in God."

Early in the 2010 season, the Eagles's starting quarterback was injured, and suddenly Michael became the starter. He took full advantage of the chance and set so many records in a game against the Redskins that the NFL Hall of Fame asked for his jersey. Then, Michael rallied the Eagles from a 21-point deficit against the Giants with only eight minutes to play in one of the most improbable comebacks in NFL history. Before the miracle comeback, Vick had already received more Pro Bowl votes than any player in the NFL.

The Eagles's win on the road over the 9–4 Giants clinched a playoff spot and positioned them as the number-two seed in the NFC. The other top NFC seed? Michael's former team, the Atlanta Falcons!

I debated for months about when to write about Michael's situation, having adopted a wait-and-see, hopeful attitude regarding his turnaround. Three situations captured my attention. First, he was all business on the field, playing with quiet humility and determination. Second, Michael spoke to kids in two dozen schools, earnestly telling them that his previous lifestyle was wrong and encouraging them to learn from his mistakes.

The third one was a humorous bit. A South Jersey Toyota dealer made a TV commercial of a salesman showing cars to Vick. When he sees Michael admiring a large SUV, the salesman directs him to the smallest car in the lot, implying, "This is a car that you can afford."

That commercial reminded viewers of Michael's financial plight. Once able to buy virtually anything his heart desired, Vick received an allowance of less than $5,000 per month, which was an extremely small amount compared to his first NFL multi-million dollar annual salary with Atlanta. His great play and good behavior ultimately earned him an unprecedented second $100 million plus contract that afforded him the opportunity to pay off all of his creditors and become debt-free.

Many people refused to forgive Vick, who is the epitome of a sandlot quarterback with his impromptu broken-field runs. Like a sandlot quarterback would, Jesus once drew a play in the dirt for the bloodthirsty Pharisees who were preparing to stone an adulterous woman (see John 8:6–11). Jesus told the Pharisees in the huddle that if one of them was without sin, "cast the first stone." Stung by Jesus's words, beginning with the eldest to the youngest, each Pharisee broke the huddle, dropped his stone, and did not return, leaving only Jesus and the adulterous woman. Jesus simply said to her, "Now go and sin no more." Jesus would likely give similar advice to the people who have still not forgiven Michael, even after he paid his debt to society and professed to be a changed man. Neither would Jesus have missed the opportunity to coach Michael, as Tony Dungy did.

I saw solid evidence of God's redemptive plan in Michael's life. Sixteen thousand hours behind bars left Michael with plenty of time to be alone with his thoughts. Michael testified, "God gave me a second chance," and he has made the most of his second chance.

Let's pray for Michael Vick's faith journey to continue. Remember that our most loving and generous God is also the God of second chances. It was our most awesome God who gave you and me the chance for redemption through his Son Jesus Christ, who was nailed to the cross.

> Prayer: Father God, I believe that Jesus Christ died for every sin, large or small, past, present, or future, so that each person can receive the cleansing power of Christ's blood that was spilled on the cross. I pray for all who are lost to accept Jesus as Savior and Lord and receive eternal life. Thank you for the mercy and grace that you give anyone who comes to you with a repentant heart. In Jesus's name, amen.

FB69:
OUR CORNERSTONE

ISAIAH 28:16, 1 PETER 2:6, MATTHEW 21:42

The stone the builders rejected has become the cornerstone;
the Lord has done this, and it is marvelous in our eyes.

—Matthew 21:42

Michael Vick spent two years in prison for his part in a dogfighting scandal. He sat in a maximum security prison, apart from his young children, owing creditors tens of millions of dollars. Tony Dungy visited him in Leavenworth on a weekly basis, and Michael turned his life around by committing it to Jesus Christ. Through the mercy and grace of God, Michael was given a second chance.

Look how things have progressed for Michael. He was named the 2010 NFL Comeback Player of the Year after leading the Eagles to the playoffs. He received an endorsement from a Christian CEO who believes in second chances. Then came the news that Michael was tendered a $20 million annual contract because the Eagles selected him as their franchise player. NFL rules state that a franchise player receives the average salary of the top five players at his position. That means the Eagles said Michael Vick is the most important player to our future and the one we cannot afford to lose. The Eagles figuratively named Michael as the cornerstone, the chief cog to build the team around.

Michael went from being rejected by society and the NFL for his shortcomings and mistakes to being the cornerstone of the Eagles franchise. He was given a chance by one team, and two years later in 2011, he became a player worth $20 million. He was on top of his profession, totally blew it, was truly repentant and committed to turn his life around through Jesus Christ, publicly admitted his sin time and time again, and climbed back to the top of his profession.

The primary reason that Michael, the cornerstone, came back is because of *the* Cornerstone, Jesus Christ. Recall that Christ was the cornerstone around which God would build his kingdom, but Jesus the Cornerstone was rejected by the Jews because he rocked their comfortable world. Christ ended up going to the cross for the sins of the Jews and everybody else then, now, and forever. Through his resurrection and ascension, Christ indeed reigns as the Chief Cornerstone of the kingdom of God. Putting your trust in the precious Cornerstone chosen by God is the only way to salvation, joy, and peace, regardless of circumstance.

> Prayer: Dear Father God, it is always a glorious thing to see one of your lost sheep come back into the fold. Thank you for the redemption of Michael Vick. Strengthen him for the battles ahead, and may he be a warrior for the kingdom of God. In Jesus's holy and precious name, amen.

FB70: INDISPUTABLE EVIDENCE

MATTHEW 16:15-16, HEBREWS 10:10

Simon Peter answered and said, 'You are the Christ, the Son of the living God.'

—Matthew 16:16

Football fans of the twenty-first century recognize the term "indisputable evidence." The term indisputable evidence originated in the NFL and was later adopted by major college football. The NFL implemented a process to review controversial calls by the officials. The purpose of the review was to ensure that the officials got the play right every time. The referee, a head coach, or the replay official in the replay booth can request a review of a play. Unless there is complete evidence that the officials on the field missed the call, the play stands. As I watch the same replay that the replay official is watching, I am surprised how often a play is allowed to stand when evidence that appears indisputable to me is viewed differently by the replay official. The process is an improvement, but it is not failproof and remains somewhat controversial.

One thing is for sure. No matter what the skeptics and atheists say, there is indisputable evidence that Jesus Christ walked on this earth, was crucified by Jews and Romans on a cross, and triumphantly rose from the grave and ascended to heaven. A former atheist and agnostic named Lee Strobel set out to prove or disprove these facts after observing the transformation that occurred in his wife's life after she received Jesus Christ as her Savior. Strobel was a professional investigative writer for the *Chicago Tribune*, so he was well schooled in how to conduct an investigation. He interviewed many Christian historians and theologians across the United States.

Lee's discovery changed his life forever. Strobel proved to himself and to many others in his classic work, *The Case for Christ*, that the prophecies contained in his grandmother's Jewish Old Testament Bible were true beyond any shadow of a doubt. Lee concluded that Jesus could not have faked his death on the cross, and that there was no impostor substituted while Jesus was whisked away stage right. He found no physical evidence that Jesus's body was stolen. Finally, there was the transformation when over ten thousand Jews suddenly gave up rituals and traditions of animal sacrifice that had been part of Jewish tradition for several thousand years, because they realized Jesus was the "once for all" Sacrifice from God (see Hebrews 10:10). All of the facts could only mean that Jesus was born to a virgin, performed miracles, and died for our sins and emerged from the grave as our risen Savior and Lord.

What evidence does each Christian have that Christ is alive? Because he lives in our hearts. And that evidence alone cannot be disputed.

> Prayer: Father God, I praise you that I can celebrate the risen Lord. Thank you for the hard evidence that Christ ascended to heaven, sits at your right hand, and lives in my heart. In Jesus's name, amen.

FB71:
EXCESSIVE CELEBRATION

2 SAMUEL 6:14-23

Then David danced before the Lord with all his might.

—2 Samuel 6:14

Football fans abhor the inconsistent way that "excessive celebration" penalties have been handed down by major college football officials. The rule is designed to prevent players from bringing undue attention to themselves and from showing up their opponents after scoring a touchdown. The rule has been controversial because of the inconsistency with which it has been implemented.

David was once accused of excessive celebration when he praised the Lord. The Scriptures record that David danced all night and even stripped down to his loins as he danced. That display caused controversy among the Jews, but David was so joyous in the Lord that he expressed that joy as God had made him.

We are born with different inner passions, and to be able to use those passions to reverently give God glory, honor, and praise is one of the great privileges and responsibilities that we have as Christians. Some people like to clap their hands or raise them in praise to our most high God during a worship service. Buckhead Church in Atlanta has a great rock band which adds modern energy to even the most traditional songs. Predominantly African

American churches often have choirs that sway with the music and the rhythms. Sacred Tapestry UMC featured jazz musicians that played classical and spiritual music to create an atmosphere that helps new churchgoers feel more comfortable. Dance troupes perform beautiful interpretative dances to honor God and bring him glory.

Whenever an expressive dance or high-energy song glorifies God and praises him, the ruling is "no penalty." However, when any form of worship crosses the line and draws undue attention to anyone other than God, it is a form of "excessive celebration."

> Prayer: Father God, I thank you that there is no one way to let you know that I love you, and that I want to give you the glory, honor, and praise. Thank you for making us unique so that we march to the drums of different beats. May our song, dance, and praise always be in reverence, love and respect for all that you have done for us. In Jesus's name, amen.

FB72:
PASSING THE TEST

1 CORINTHIANS 10:13, JAMES 1

No temptation has overtaken you except such as is common to man; but God is faithful, who will not allow you to be tempted beyond what you are able, but with the temptation will also make the way of escape, that you may be able to bear it.

—1 Corinthians 10:13

In the 2012 SEC Championship game, Alabama defeated Georgia 32–28 when the Bulldogs ran out of time inside the Alabama five. The Georgia Dome atmosphere was absolutely electric throughout the game as the crowd, evenly divided between Bulldog and Tide supporters, roared on every play. It was the most exciting game that I had witnessed since the 1982 Georgia–Penn State national championship game. The combination of intensity and high level of play made this contest the de facto national championship game for me.

Thirty years had passed since Georgia had played for a chance to go to the title game. The defeat was an incredibly bitter pill to swallow for the Georgia team, especially for the two people who had received the most criticism from the press. Head Coach Mark Richt and quarterback Aaron Murray had been unfairly singled out for Georgia's inability to "win the big game," and it came to a head in the postgame press conference.

On the Thursday before the game, I listened to an afternoon sports talk radio segment on 680 The Fan in Atlanta. Talk show co-hosts Chuck Oliver and Matt Chernoff played an audio tape of a spirited exchange between a *Los Angeles Times* reporter and UCLA Bruins Coach Jim Mora Jr. The reporter triggered the debate by implying that Mora's team gave less than their best effort against Stanford so that UCLA could play Stanford instead of Oregon in the upcoming Pac-12 Championship game.

Doggone if Oliver didn't pull the same stunt with Coach Richt immediately after the toughest loss of his twelve-year career at UGA! At the SEC postgame press conference, Oliver asked Coach Richt to respond to "people saying" that he and Aaron Murray fail to deliver in the biggest games on the biggest stages. Despite being blindsided, somehow Coach Richt kept his composure. After leaving the press conference, Coach Richt quickly returned to the room to emphasize what a great effort Aaron Murray and the team had given, and that it was "unbelievable" if anybody thinks otherwise. Way to go, Coach!

On Sunday morning, Becca and I were discussing if God tests people by the outcome of games. In my opinion, this reporter's agenda was to "draw Coach Richt offside" and bring him outside his Christian character. The exchange was a huge test for Richt, who had been under the brightest spotlight of his career during the past four hours.

He could have verbally ripped the reporter's nose off his face (which might have been my reaction!). If he rips the reporter, people all over the country who don't know Christ could say, "Oh, listen to him, he's supposed to be such a big Christian!" Instead, he handled the criticism with commendable tact and composure. Paul wrote in 1 Corinthians 10:13, "No temptation has overtaken you except such as is common to man; but God is faithful, who will not allow you to be tempted beyond what you are able, but with the temptation will also make the way of escape, that you may be able to bear it."

Ever since Georgia's win over Florida in November, I had a recurring picture in my mind of Coach Richt hoisting the crystal football after the BCS National Championship game in Miami. I envisioned this incredible platform for Christ that he would have in the endless interviews during the five weeks leading up to the BCS game against Notre Dame. Well, that's not how it worked out, is it?

Instead, Coach Richt suddenly gets put on the spot by a copy-cat reporter. Here was a perfect chance to fall flat on his face on ESPN. Well, he didn't, did he? With his direct but poised reply, Mark passed the test, withstanding the same type of temptation that we face when we are unfairly treated or unjustly accused. Deceptions such as the one used by the reporter are nothing new. "The serpent deceived me, and I ate" (Genesis 3:13). We are warned in 1 Peter 5:8 to be ready, to "be sober-minded; be watchful. Your adversary...prowls around like a roaring lion, seeking someone to devour."

There is a great reward that awaits Christians who come through in the clutch for God. James 1:12 reminds us that "blessed is the man who endures temptation; for when he has been approved, he will receive the crown of life which the Lord has promised to those who love Him." James 1:13–14 also instructs us, "Let no one say when he is tempted, 'I am tempted by God'; for God cannot be tempted by evil, or does he himself tempt anyone. But each one is tempted when he is drawn away by his own desires and enticed."

Now here is a really tough one for me. I am supposed to count these tests of my faith all as joy? "Count it all joy, my brothers, when you meet trials of various kinds, for you know that the testing of your faith produces steadfastness. And let steadfastness have its full effect, that you may be perfect and complete, lacking in nothing" (James 1:2–4). Passing these tests is exactly how we grow in obedience and our faith in God.

I said, "It's great! To be! A Georgia Bulldog!" I'm proud of our head coach who stood up for his quarterback, his team, and himself in a way that honored Christ!

> Prayer: Most Holy God, help me pass the tests that come my way. When I refuse to cave into the ploys of the evil one, I bring glory and honor to you. In the name of Jesus, amen.

FB73:
WHERE IS GOD ON YOUR
TEN-POINT SCALE?

EXODUS 20:3, ISAIAH 45:5,
MATTHEW 16:26, JOHN 3:30

You shall have no other gods before me.

—Exodus 20:3

I read a wonderful book called *God and Football* by Chad Gibbs. Gibbs was a rabid Alabama fan as a teenager who then enrolled at Auburn, where he switched football allegiances to the chagrin of some family members. In the fall of 2009, for twelve consecutive weeks, Gibbs attended a football game on a different SEC campus. He really captured the unique aspects of each campus and city. What made his book unique was that he interviewed local Christian football fans each weekend to find out how they balanced their faith and fanaticism for SEC football. He attended a worship service for twelve different denominations in twelve different cities.

Gibbs discovered that many fans get too carried away with their team's performance. The book highlights how selfish desires overtake our devotion to God and leave him in second place. One of the most insightful observations came from a pastor who acknowledged that God made us to be passionate about certain things, and for millions of fans in the South, that means he made us to be fervent about following our favorite college football teams. A key takeaway is that God expects us to balance our passion for sports as we grow in our faith.

When I hear my favorite rock anthems from the 1970s, I still really get into them. I can't help it. It's who I am, and it's a passion that God gave me. But too many times, either the music or Georgia football or Kentucky basketball or golf or other selfish desires have taken on too much importance. The danger is when I cross the line, and God slips to second place or lower and stays out of first place for longer than I care to admit. I'm not talking about the three hours when I scream my lungs out for my favorite team to win. It's in the aftermath of a thrilling comeback win or especially a tough loss. Will I "get over it" in five minutes or five hours or five days? If I am still in the dumps after several days, something is askew in my relationship with Christ.

Certainly, it's great fun cheering for your team and hanging with the fans after a big win. But did your favorite team promise to never leave you nor forsake you? In the movie *Fever Pitch*, Ben's friend asked him after Ben lamented that each season his beloved Red Sox always broke his heart, "When have they ever loved you back?

When has your team stood by you and your family through thick or thin? Who loved you so much that he gave his only Son to die for your sins so that you could have eternal life? It surely wasn't your team or your other little gods, who have never cared about you and never loved you back.

If your passion for your team or favorite sport is an eight or nine on a scale of one to ten, that's cool. God doesn't expect you to smother your enthusiasm and dial it back to a four. But we should strive for our devotion to God to be a ten, keeping him ahead of all other passions to maintain right standing with him. "You shall have no other gods before me" (Exodus 20:3).

We wouldn't really give up everything for a national championship, would we? "For what profit is it to a man if he gains the whole world and loses his own soul" (Matthew 16:26)? It's a daily battle with the enemy and self to keep God first in our lives. "He must increase, and I must decrease" (John 3:30). In our spiritual life, God should always be in first place and our champion.

> Prayer: Dear Lord, I am so grateful for your perfect love. May I keep you first in my words, deeds, and actions. In the name of the risen Son, amen.

FB74:
JESUS AND GOD
ARE ALWAYS THERE

PROVERBS 18:24, MATTHEW 26:69-75, HEBREWS 13:5, 8

Jesus Christ is the same yesterday, today, and forever.

—Hebrews 13:8 (KJV)

Quarterback Eli Manning and his New York Giant teammates were heralded as conquerors after winning the 2008 Super Bowl in an improbable walk through the playoffs as a wild card. The team brought back memories of the powerful Giant teams of the early 1960s and the 1986 Super Bowl winner led by Head Coach Bill Parcells and quarterback Phil Simms. Eli led his team to a Super Bowl victory and joined his brother Peyton as the only brothers to quarterback Super Bowl champions.

But Eli Manning knows how far the drop can be from the height of his profession after this experience in 2010. Eli showed up for a Tuesday press conference to discuss the previous Sunday's game with the Eagles. The Giants led 31–10 at Giants Stadium with only eight minutes to play, but the Eagles engineered a truly improbable comeback, scoring four touchdowns in regulation time. The last touchdown came on a sixty-five-yard punt return on the last play of the game.

Eli walked into the press room to face the reporters and take their questions, but there were no reporters! Usually there would have been ten to twenty reporters anxious to ask questions and get the inside scoop on the upcoming game. Apparently, the media was so fed up with the Giants blowing the game that they just pulled a no-show.

Sometimes, we may feel like everyone has deserted us. Jesus knows exactly how it feels to be deserted. First, Judas Escariot squealed on him to the chief priests. Then he was abandoned by Peter (see Matthew 26:69–75) and his other disciples (except John) as he hung from the cross. But for those reasons, you can rest assured that Jesus will always show up for you, no matter how well or how poorly you've played. God himself promised that he will never leave us nor abandon us. Proverbs 18:24 reminds us that some people will pretend to be our friends, but there is a friend who sticks right there with us at all times, even closer than a brother. His name is Jesus, and he will always be there for us.

> Prayer: Father God, I want to totally trust in your promises. I choose to live by faith that you are always there when I need you because you have never failed to be there yet. In the name of Jesus, amen.

FB75:
DAILY WORKOUTS

PHILIPPIANS 2:12-16

You must work out your own salvation in fear and trembling. For it is God who works in you, inspiring both the will and the deed, for his chosen purpose.

—Philippians 2:12–13

Daily workouts are an important regimen for any professional athlete. A top-flight athlete will hire a personal trainer who tailors a program that enables the athlete to achieve peak physical condition. Because each athlete's body is unique and different physical attributes need to be developed for a particular sport, the workout regimen will vary from athlete to athlete.

Gaining maximum efficiency comes down to how much effort an athlete is willing to put into his daily workout. How much of a price is an athlete willing to pay to achieve his or her goals? I recall NFL Hall of Fame running back Walter Payton inviting his pro football friends to join him for an off-season workout. They were about to find out why Walter Payton became the all-time leading rusher in NFL history while never suffering a major injury. He took them to the sandy levees of his native Mississippi delta. On a broiling hot summer afternoon, Walter challenged them to complete his daily routine of running up the steep slopes. Their feet bogged down in the sand, creating huge footprints.

It was a major exertion to walk these steep slopes, much less to run wind sprints! All of them dropped out, and some lost their lunches in the process. Meanwhile, Walter churned out sprints in the scorching heat.

It's important that we put in daily workouts to grow in our faith and draw closer to God. We're all different, so one size will not fit all. Some may gravitate to reading the Bible, and some will enjoy reading devotions with Bible verses. Still others are naturally drawn to prayer and meditation, and others may be drawn to spiritual music. All of our efforts should honor and worship God. What is important is that you find your daily regimen that will allow you to withstand the enemy by putting on the armor of God.

You must determine the time and effort that you put into your daily spiritual workout. Your time will vary day to day, depending on your schedule. It doesn't always have to be the same daily Bible reading and prayer routine. Athletes will vary their daily workouts. They will run one day and lift the next day to give specific muscles a chance to rest.

I realize that athletes are paid to work out several hours a day and have tons of free time that you may not have with a busy work or school schedule and family commitments. But God will honor the time that we can carve out of our days, even if it's fifteen minutes in the morning or evening. God will bless us when we intentionally connect with him daily. You may surprise yourself by reaching spiritual discipline goals that you didn't believe were possible. Be faithful to the daily spiritual tasks, and give God the glory, honor, and praise for the people and situations that he brings you as a result of your dedication to worship.

Prayer: Dear Lord, thank you for meeting me when I carve out time for you. May I show you how much your love and forgiveness mean to me. In Jesus's name, amen.

FB76:
THE GREEN DOT

ROMANS 8:26-39

The Holy Spirit helps us with our daily problems.

—Romans 8:26 (TLB)

An increase in domed stadiums, which hold much more noise than open-air stadiums, placed a greater burden on the NFL quarterbacks. In 2006, the NFL placed a tiny receiver in the helmet of the quarterback to help him receive plays from the offensive coordinator. A green dot marks any helmet with the special communications device. The device allows one-way communication to the quarterback from the offensive coordinator during the first twenty-five seconds on the play clock. Two years later, the league installed the same device in the helmet of a defensive player. Usually, an inside linebacker, who is the quarterback of the defense, wears the green-dot helmet. These devices allow the teams to execute the correct play more frequently with fewer false starts.

Sometimes, we don't execute the play that God wants because we aren't listening. Through the Holy Spirit, we have access to his inner voice that tells us what to do, but we don't stop long enough to listen. Some might say that it's an audible voice, but most of us would say that it is inaudible. It takes being connected with God through the Holy Spirit to sense that little voice that comes in the form of a thought. The next time God speaks to you through your "receiver in a helmet" and gives you sound guidance, act on his advice and remember to thank him!

> Prayer: Most holy God, thank you for the messages that you send me through that inner voice that only I can detect. May I be ever mindful of your direction and suggestions and follow through on them. In the name of Jesus, amen.

FB77:
SALVATION SCHOLARSHIP

JOHN 6:37, ACTS 20:24, EPHESIANS 4:30

The one who comes to Me I will by no means cast out.

—John 6:37

In 2011, Becca read the beginning of an online article to me that made my stomach churn. "Arkansas has granted scholarship releases to two more players from its football program in offensive lineman Cam Feldt and linebacker Austin Moss…The players are the fourth and fifth to be released this week as coaches perform annual scholarship evaluations."

Annual scholarship evaluations? To borrow NFL analyst Keyshawn Johnson's catchphrase, c'mon man! A player can be rightfully released from his scholarship for reasons such as academic shortcomings and personal misconduct. But it is evident that players are released because they aren't considered to be good enough. Their scholarships are taken away and given to incoming freshmen and junior college transfers.

FBS scholarships are renewable year to year, but it has long been a gentleman's agreement that a player who signed with a major university could expect to stay on scholarship for either four or five years (redshirt). He could at least trot out to meet his parents on Senior Day if he held up his end of the agreement.

Apparently, this is no longer the case at some institutions. I doubt any recruiter has ever told a hot prospect, "Son, come play for us, and at the end of your freshman and sophomore years, we will let you know if we are going to renew your scholarship or give it to a player who can help us more than you can."

It's a blessing for believers that our "salvation scholarships" don't depend on us being good enough each year. How chilling it would be if God reviewed our credentials each year on May 1. What if he looked at how often we had shared our faith or reached out to others in need in the past twelve months? Based on those results, he would decide whether or not to pull our "salvation scholarships." Of course, God would never do that, but he does expect us to bear fruit for the kingdom. The apostle Paul said, "Life is worth nothing unless I use it for doing the work assigned me by the Lord Jesus, the work of telling others the good news about God's mighty kindness and love" (Acts 20:24). Jesus said, "The one who comes to me, I will by no means cast out" (John 6:37). How blessed we are that once we've been covered with the forgiveness of the blood of the Lamb that we are immediately "sealed by the Holy Spirit" (Ephesians 4:30) for eternity with God. Satan can never take away our salvation, but he will try to keep us from helping others join God's team of believers.

I wonder if some big-time football coaches can truthfully say, "The ones who play for me, I will by no means release them unjustly from their scholarships."

> Prayer: Father God, it is such a blessing that I do not have to earn your grace which you freely gave me through Christ dying for my sin on the cross and rising from the dead. May I return the blessing by being ever diligent to block and tackle daily for your kingdom. In the Holy and Precious name of Our Lord and Savior, Amen.

FB78:
YOU REALLY NEED
TO GET THAT SEEN ABOUT

PSALM 139:23-24, ROMANS 7:14-25

For we know that the law is spiritual, but I am carnal, sold under sin.

—Romans 7:14

I transferred to the University of Georgia for my junior and senior years along with my friends Mike and Joel. One of the most fun things that we found that first semester was playing touch football on the UGA Astroturf practice field. After the football team completed practice, we would play touch football games or kick field goals. It was great fun because turf made you run a little faster and cut a little sharper.

Unfortunately, I discovered a downside to Astroturf after I dove for a pass and scraped my forearm on the turf. Several days later, my arm swelled and, using male college student intuitive logic, I thought that it would eventually heal on its own.

Joel walked in from class one day and saw my swollen forearm, which had now developed sores and looked a lot like Popeye's. He looked me in the eye and said sternly, "You really need to get that seen about."

I went to the UGA health clinic the following morning. Sure enough, I had a staph infection. The nurse lanced my arm and bandaged it heavily. Fortunately, I recovered completely in several weeks and thankfully have never had another problem.

How often does sin come into our lives, establish a toehold, and become a stronghold? When we fail to confront our sin head on, the sin becomes so dominant that others can see what we are ignoring, like I ignored the fact that I needed to address my swollen arm. You don't recognize what sin is doing to you!

Look at yourself. Is there a sin dominating your life that others recognize? It could be sixty-hour work weeks that leave you drained, impatient, and solely focused on your job. Perhaps an idol in your life has taken you away from God. Whatever it is, don't let someone else point it out. Allow the Holy Spirit to search your heart for unconfessed sin (see Psalm 139:24). Be in prayer daily, read your Bible, and allow the Holy Spirit to give you discernment to spot your sin and the courage to confront any sin that has severed your relationship with God and Jesus Christ.

> Prayer: Holy Spirit, please help me find every sin that has separated me from God and from Jesus. Give me the strength and determination to confront it, confess it, and get right with the three of you. In the name of our precious Messiah, amen.

FB79:
GOAL-LINE STAND

MATTHEW 26:39-44; 27:26, 31-33, 35-50; 28:1-6

He is not here, for he is risen as he said. Come, see the place where the Lord lay.

—Matthew 28:6

I shared a message with the West Laurens High School football team. This opportunity was a special honor because I participated on the first West Laurens varsity sports teams exactly forty years before in 1971–72. My brother L. E.'s church provided a pregame meal for the players and coaches, and our good friend, Pastor Greg Lowery, invited me to share with the team. I umpired Greg's summer baseball games and remember his wicked sidearm fastball. Here is an excerpt of my message to the team.

> Remember those long, hot, painful practices in August. Think about the temperature that felt well over one hundred degrees inside your sweaty helmets as you strained to complete the last gasser of the day and hoped you didn't have to throw up in the trash can. Remember how you made it, only to get to come back the next day and do it all over again.
>
> Why did the coaches put you and your teammates through such pain and agony? So that you won't quit tonight in the fourth quarter. So that you will be stronger

than your opponent when the game is on the line. So that you and your teammates can be in a position to make a goal line stand that you will remember for the rest of your days.

Nothing lifts the spirit of a football team and its fans like a fourth-quarter goal-line stand. With each stop the defense makes to keep the opponent out of the end zone, the crowd gets louder and goes crazy when the fourth down stop is made. One of the most famous fourth down stops happened in the 1979 Sugar Bowl. Alabama held Penn State out of the end zone from inside the one on the first three downs. On fourth down, Alabama linebacker Barry Krauss met the Penn State tailback in midair and stopped him inches from the goal line to preserve the 14–7 win. The collision was so violent that Krauss knocked himself out and suffered severe headaches for several days following the game. Krauss's heroic play, which was made possible by his interior line jamming the blocking, became one of the legends in Alabama football history. The play was nicknamed Gut Check. Paintings and photographs of number 77 making the game-saving tackle still adorn the walls in family rooms and dens from Mobile to Double Springs.

Very late in the fourth quarter of his thirty-three-year life on earth, Jesus Christ made the eternal version of the most incredible four-play, goal-line stand of all time. On first down, Jesus knelt in the Garden of Gethsemane in the middle of the night, praying fervently to come to grips with the destiny that he would die within hours for the sins of all mankind. He prayed to God that the Father's will would be accomplished. Jesus prayed so intensely that capillaries in his forehead burst, splattering drops of blood at his feet.

On second down, Pontius Pilate, the Roman governor, turned Jesus over to the Roman army for a whipping that was called scourging. Christ was given thirty-nine incredibly painful lashes by the soldiers who used whips that were laced with bone fragments. The whips ripped Jesus's flesh so deeply that his bones were exposed, and Jesus bled profusely as his body became raw flesh.

On third down, the soldiers forced a ravaged, blood-soaked Jesus to carry and drag a heavy cross hundreds of yards down the Via Dolorosa in Jerusalem. When Jesus stumbled from the weight of the cross, a Roman solider grabbed a man named Simeon of Cyrene and forced him to help Jesus carry the cross to Golgotha.

On fourth down, Jesus was nailed to that cross and crucified. The Son of Man summoned every ounce of courage, determination, and heart, and survived six grueling hours in excruciating pain as he painfully gasped for each breath. How did Jesus make it through these four downs? It was simply because of his infinite and perfect love for us that he died for our sins, making it possible for us to be united in heaven with Jesus and God for eternity.

The tiny remnant of Christ's followers that witnessed his death was surely convinced that the eternal game was lost. But God resurrected Jesus from the dead on the third day! When several of his female followers found the tomb to be empty on Easter morning, they rejoiced! The eternal goal-line stand had worked, and Christ had defeated death forever!

> Prayer: Dear Father, thank you for the indescribable courage of Jesus to fulfill the prophecies in such an incredibly painful way. Thank you for your gift of our Savior and Lord who beat death so that I too can claim victory over death. In the precious name of Jesus Christ, amen.

FB80:
GOAL-LINE STAND SEQUEL

1 SAMUEL 15:1-26, LUKE 2:42-49, JOHN 6:38

Behold, to obey is better than sacrifice.

—1 Samuel 15:22

Before I gave my talk to the West Laurens Raiders at my brother's church, I asked some boys at one table who their quarterback was. They pointed me to a table in the back corner where some seniors were sitting.

I introduced myself to the senior quarterback named Kaleeb Stanley and struck up a conversation. He told me that after his senior year, he hoped to attend a military college, and he had his eye on The Citadel. I asked Kaleeb, "If you were the quarterback, what would you do if you were up by two points with thirty seconds left in the game, and you had the ball?" I had already decided that he would say, "Take a knee," because that's what teams should do.

Instead, with no hesitation, Kaleeb stopped eating, looked at me, and confidently said, "I would do whatever my coach told me to do." Wow! He is obviously an experienced quarterback, but I was so impressed that he would do whatever his coach told him to do. How is that for being in sync with your coach?

That evening, West Laurens pulled off what one blogger described as the "upset of the decade," defeating third-ranked Class AAA opponent Peach County, 21–14. The loss snapped a twenty-nine-game Peach winning streak. West Laurens Head Coach Stacy Nobles told me before the game that his team had a chance if they could avoid beating themselves in the first quarter as they had done in their two losses. Kaleeb ran the offense expertly with no costly turnovers. His good friend at his table, Demetrius Green, who was excited about running a 4.39 forty-yard dash the previous day, rushed for a career-high 244 yards.

Recall the story of King Saul receiving marching orders from the prophet Samuel to utterly destroy the Amalekites. King Saul failed to follow God's orders to the letter, and God promptly stripped him of his kingship. Samuel said, "You have rejected the word of the Lord, and the Lord has rejected you from being king over Israel" (1 Samuel 15:26). In God's eyes, Saul had been both rebellious and stubborn by not wiping out the opposing king and his choice head of cattle.

Recall how twelve-year-old Jesus said that he needed to be about his father's business (Luke 2:42–49). He often said that he came to do his Father's work and to do what his Father told him to do. Jesus is one of the three forms of the Godhead that make up the Holy Trinity, and certainly, he was capable of making the correct decisions on his own because Jesus is perfect. But he always chose to follow his father's guidance, because to Jesus it was first and foremost about obedience. "For I have come down from heaven, not to do my own will, but the will of him who sent me" (John 6:38).

Often we make decisions, believing we know what to do, but it may not be the best thing for us, or it may not be in step with God's plan. For each of us, it should be about obedience, which is the best gift that we can give God. How can we know we are being obedient? Before making an important decision, we can consult Scripture, pray to God about it, listen for his inner voice to guide us, and discuss it with a brother or sister in Christ. If these options all line up, we can have confidence that our decision is in line with God's direction.

Even when he knew what to do late in the game, Kaleeb would check with his coach for guidance. My final thought regarding Kaleeb is that this young man will make one tremendous soldier for America!

> Prayer: Dear Lord, thank you for this awesome example of obedience from a young man who is in tune with his coach. May I be in tune with you just as closely as that young man was with his coach. In Jesus's name, amen.

FB81:
THE WINNING SIDE

ROMANS 6:23, EPHESIANS 2:8-9, 4:30

The wages of sin is death, but the gift of God is eternal life through Jesus Christ.

—Romans 6:23

Becca and I attended the 2011 UGA–UT Game in Knoxville. Neyland Stadium is a huge stadium that holds over one hundred thousand fans with an upper deck that extends completely around the stadium. Neyland Stadium can get really loud because the sound cannot escape as it does in open-ended stadiums. Georgia played very well and escaped with a 20–12 victory to our delight. Even though some people left the game early, traffic was still a nightmare, and we wearily pulled into our motel just before 1:00 a.m. early Sunday morning.

When I woke up the next morning, I immediately thought of the game, and the fact that we were on the winning side. It surely beat the bad feeling the last time we were on the road to watch a sporting event. Back in April 2011, we were in Houston having watched Kentucky, our other favorite team, lose in the basketball Final Four. I remember waking up the next morning, immediately remembering the loss and realizing we had thirteen long hours to drive back to Atlanta so that Jillian could be at work on Monday morning.

I also realized that no matter how my team performs the night before, I will always wake up on the winning side for eternity! What a reassuring thought it is to know that I am safe with the Lord, and that after I go to sleep here on earth for the last time, I am guaranteed heaven. No matter how lousy things are going at work or school, there is no switching sides after you have committed your heart to Christ through repentance of your sin and placing your trust in him.

Prayer: Father God, I praise you for the day that I joined your eternal winning side and for the hope that I have no matter how things are going here on earth. Help me through this day with the confidence and assurance that you are with me now and will be with me forever. In the holy name of Jesus, amen.

FB82:
THE RED ZONE

LUKE 9:23

And He said to them all, if any man will come after Me, let him deny himself, and take up his cross daily, and follow Me. (KJV)

The red zone in football is the area from the opponent's twenty-yard line to the end zone. The effectiveness of an offensive team is measured by the percentage of touchdowns scored inside the red zone. A percentage of seventy-five is considered to be excellent, while fifty percent or less leaves much to be desired. It's more difficult to advance across the goal line inside the ten, and it is most difficult inside the five. Even though the distance is shorter, it's like running uphill versus a flat surface. It takes more effort to score a touchdown because the eleven defenders are all bunched up. Safeties that normally play twenty yards off the ball are now five to ten yards from the ball.

In our Christian lives, surrendering the last five to ten percent of our lives is the most difficult. I surrender *all* is how the song goes. It doesn't say I will surrender most of it. By taking up our crosses and following Christ daily (see Luke 9:23) in every aspect of our lives, we become totally free to allow God to really use us to further his kingdom. Satan senses when we are getting close, and he will fight us like a dog to hold onto the last bit of the red zone. If the enemy can defend the red zone, he can keep some people that we know out of heaven.

Perhaps your red zone is a secret sin, alcohol, your work, an idol in your life such as your favorite football team, television, or the Internet. Whatever is keeping God out of that area of your life, God cannot *really* use you until you surrender. When you surrender, God will carry you triumphantly into the end zone, and the change in you can make the difference between winning and losing for many people. It can be the difference between people that you know either going to heaven or spending eternity in the abyss, separated from God forever.

> Prayer: Father God, thank you for never giving up on me and for continuing to coach me until I surrender it all to you. In Jesus's name, amen.

FB83:
WORRY? WHO, ME?

PROVERBS 3:5-6, MATTHEW 6:25-33, 1 PETER 5:7

Therefore do not worry, saying, 'What shall we eat?' or 'What shall we drink?' or 'What shall we wear?' For after all these things, the Gentiles seek. For your heavenly Father knows that you need all these things. But seek first the kingdom of God and his righteousness, and all these things shall be added to you.

—Matthew 6:31–33

Hall of Fame broadcaster Larry Munson was the beloved, legendary voice of the Georgia Bulldogs for forty years. He was well known for his great calls in famous Bulldog victories, such as "Oh, you, Herschel Walker!" and "Oh, look at the sugar falling from the sky!" Dawg fans will never forget, "Lindsay Scott! Lindsay Scott! Lindsay Scott!"

Larry was also known in the Georgia camp for being the biggest worrier about the upcoming game on Saturday afternoon. Even during the glory days of Herschel Walker, Larry was always fretting that the wind would blow too hard out of the north and bother the kicking game, or some second-string tackle wasn't going to be available, or the team bus would break down on the way to the stadium.

During the week, he would interview Vince Dooley, who was always cautious about his team's chances. While speaking with Coach Dooley, he would wind Vince up, and Dooley would become even more pessimistic about his team's chances on Saturday.

Do you know a believer who, even when things are going well, can usually find something to worry about? The bad habit doesn't make a person any less of a Christian, but it can certainly dim his or her light and cause anxiety, stress, and churn in that believer's life.

If you consider yourself a worrier, think about this approach when you start to worry incessantly about a potential problem. What is the worst thing that could happen if you don't know how to handle a situation in the classroom or at work? You would be embarrassed and receive negative feedback which you could learn from. That's about it.

If you struggle in this area, I encourage you to start making bullets of your worries in a journal. If you're worried about three things, write them down and convert the three worries into prayers. Pray specifically for God to see you through each of these issues. Then ask him to help you tackle the problems. Put a little star by them when the problem gets resolved. After several weeks, you should have numerous stars along with a positive reinforcement that God is truly taking care of you and "watching over everything that concerns you" (1 Peter 5:7, TLB).

The real issue comes down to this simple question. Do we believe in Jesus or *believe* Jesus? In the sixth chapter of Matthew (25–33), Jesus told us not to worry about tomorrow, because if the sparrows have food and water, he will give us, whom he loves so much more dearly, just what we need. He makes the lilies of the field beautiful, so what won't he do for us? He will do for us what we need when we need it. Worry won't add a day to our lives, but it does make our hair grayer, can increase our blood pressure, and could even shorten our lives due to stress-related illnesses.

Worry is a sin and demonstrates a lack of trust in God. When worry dominates our thoughts, we cannot shine our light for the kingdom of God. When we convert our worries to prayers and trust God with the outcome, he will restore us.

Pastor Tim Paulk shared a story about a woman who was dressed shabbily and sold flowers to make a meager income. When she was asked why she was so positive, she said that she gives God three days to fix her problems because God fixed the biggest problem ever when he raised Jesus from the dead on the third day! Remember to thank God each time a morning worry simply vanishes by the end of the day.

> Prayer: Father God and most gracious Lord, I want to trust you and believe you. Help me come to you in prayer whenever I start to do that worry thing. When I give you a worry, I'm not coming back for it no matter what, because I trust you, Lord. In Jesus's name, amen.

FB84:
YOUR BFF

PROVERBS 18:24, ROMANS 3:23, HEBREWS 13:5, 8

There are friends who pretend to be friends, but there is a
Friend who sticks closer than a brother.

—Proverbs 18:24

Has an athlete or team ever let you down when they lose? In
2008, my Georgia Bulldogs were ranked preseason number one.
The Bulldogs won the first three games of the season, including a
late Saturday night win at Arizona State. The Dawgs would face
Alabama the following Saturday night. ESPN GameDay was in
Athens, and there was another "blackout" scheduled like the one
that was so effective against Auburn in 2007. Everything pointed
to the Dawgs winning except for one thing. The Dawgs forgot
to show up. Bama drove the length of the field for an opening
touchdown, and it was 31–0 at the half. I turned to the fellow
next to me and said, "I'm glad that I only paid $100 for this
ticket." We had put the Dawgs on a pedestal, but they crashed
and burned before our eyes, either due to the pressure of expectations, or because the West Coast game sapped their energy with
one less day to prepare, or because a tough opponent thoroughly
outplayed them.

Has a team or anyone ever disappointed you or let you down?
Everyone that we know will disappoint us in some way because

we are all imperfect human beings. The Bible teaches us that "all have sinned and fallen short of the glory of God" (Romans 3:23). The person that lets you down could be your friend, your mom or dad, brother or sister, aunt or uncle, classmate, teammate, neighbor, a favorite athlete, or favorite sports team. Perhaps a friend forgot your birthday or said something rude and hurt your feelings. Some people will hurt our feelings more than others, making us feel very badly.

When you make somebody, or something, more important than Christ in your heart, the deeper is the hurt that you feel when that person or thing disappoints you. Sometimes, you become very sad, or feel rejected, or feel like there is little hope that things will improve.

But there is always hope no matter what! The hope is the Friend who will never let us down. That Friend is God through a personal relationship with his Son, Jesus Christ. God promised that he will never leave us nor forsake us (see Hebrews 13:5), and God and Jesus are the same "yesterday, today, and forever" (Hebrews 13:8, KJV).

God loves us perfectly every moment of every day. He is loving you perfectly right now! His love is so great that it cannot be measured, and his love lasts forever. God's love will always be stronger than the love that any person can give. No one understands the depth of God's love, which was best illustrated through the life of Jesus Christ, the Son of God and Son of Man. I imagine God saying to Jesus, "I need you to live among our people and experience every hurt and rejection that they will ever feel. Then I need you to demonstrate the depth of our love by dying an incredibly painful death on a cross for their sins." Jesus loved those people who came before us, and loves us, so much that he carried out his Father's plan perfectly. You can trust God completely.

Who is our BFF—Best Friend Forever—who sticks closer than a brother? It is Jesus Christ, our Savior and Lord.

Prayer: Father God, thank you for your perfect promise that you will never forsake me. May I place Christ at the center of my life and know that Jesus has already experienced exactly what I'm going through. May I rest in your perfect love for comfort, solace, and healing from my disappointments. In Jesus's name I pray, amen.

FB85:
HAND JESUS A BLANK CHECK

EZEKIEL 36:24-27

A new heart I will give you, and a new spirit I will put within you.

—Ezekiel 36:26

I heard a saying from the NFL during the 1970s that was called forty for sixty. There were forty players on a pro football team, and the game was sixty minutes on the scoreboard clock. The saying meant that each member of the forty-man team was to give 100 percent effort for all sixty minutes.

Think about what would happen if only a portion gave maximum effort, or if all of the players only gave seventy-five percent effort and played hard for three quarters. Teams would be less successful, and fans would recognize it when players didn't give their all. The players should put their heart and soul into every play of every quarter.

Coaches recognize who is not giving their all blocking and tackling and carrying out assignments by looking at game film. God recognizes when we don't give it our all. We cannot fool God.

I remember as a young boy when my mom would sign a blank check and give it to me to take to the store or the barbershop. What fun it would have been to fill out the check for $500 and buy something amazing like a new set of golf clubs! But my mom trusted me to do what was right, and I knew I couldn't get away with it. She showed faith in me that I would wind up where I was supposed to be, use the check for its intended purpose, and write it for the intended amount. Perhaps you've had similar thoughts when your mother let you swipe the debit card.

Jesus wants you to trust him with your whole heart and give him complete reign over your life. Pretend that you were given a check that is made payable to Jesus Christ, but the space for the amount is blank. Where you normally write the amount of money in script, you write, "My whole heart." Too many times, we refuse to turn over parts of our hearts and lives to Jesus. After I received Christ, it was three years before I realized that Jesus only had 75 percent of my heart. I insisted on doing things my way in the workplace. I had not made a commitment to include God in my business dealings. God used a very painful situation that eventually brought me to my knees as I begged him to help me. I realized that I couldn't make it through a very challenging work relationship with a supervisor without him. I learned the hard way when it could have been much easier.

I created this facsimile of a blank check and inscribed "My whole heart," payable to "The One who took my place." Is it time that you signed that blank check and gave your whole heart to Christ, to let him mold and shape you in all facets of your life?

> Prayer: Most gracious God, give me the courage and commitment to allow Christ to mold me and shape every single part of my life. Give me the faith to "let go and let God" work freely in me. In Jesus's holy name, amen.

THE BLANK CHECK MADE PAYABLE TO JESUS CHRIST

316

Date: _____ , 20___

Pay to the
Order of *Jesus Christ* _____ My Whole Heart

My Sins Paid in Full by the One Who Took My Place _____

The Bank of Our Heavenly Father
Located in Heaven

For: All of My Sins   Signed: _____
['14600316 3205162820']

In what parts of my life do I need to allow Christ to become Lord?

_____
_____
_____
_____
_____
_____
_____

FB86:
EVERYBODY'S GONNA KNOW ABOUT US GOIN' AROUND!

PROVERBS 10:14, JAMES 3:1-8

A wise man holds his tongue. Only a fool blurts everything he knows; that only leads to sorrow and trouble.

—Proverbs 10:14 (TLB)

The University of Georgia played the University of Tennessee in
Knoxville in September 1980. I met Becca that summer, and we
quickly fell in love. She was a big sports fan like me, and with her
Kentucky upbringing, we both loved to beat Tennessee. I eagerly
looked forward to taking her to Knoxville with me for the opening game.

We had no tickets, which was my typical modus operandi, so
I dragged her up and down the hills of the UT campus. I bought
two from a Georgia fan and resold them to impress my new girl-
friend (which was a silly thing to do). After more searching, I
bought two uppers on the thirty-yard line in the UT alumni section from a young UT couple.

It was a miserable beginning for the Dawgs, who had the jit-
ters from the opening kickoff in front of ninety-five thousand
fans, the largest crowd they would ever see. Tennessee led 15–0

late in the third quarter when Georgia got the break they needed on a fumbled punt by Bill Bates. Here is how the legendary Georgia broadcaster Larry Munson described the play.

> *Gonna come down inside the forty, and we hit him. He fumbled the ball! A Dawg missed it; it's rolling—the ten, the seven, the five. We fumble it, we fumble it again! It's on the back of the end zone, get on that ball! We had two men miss it. We landed on it with our chests; we landed on it with our heads! Now they argue who got it as it went out of bounds!*

As the officials sorted out the play, there was a little debate brewing in my section. I leaped to my feet and shouted to Becca, "That's a safety! Tennessee is gonna have to kick to us."

The gentleman to my immediate left calmly said, "No, that's a touchback."

I whirled toward him and said, "No, it's not! That's a safety!"

His demeanor changed. Perhaps I had insulted him in front of his friends. For whatever reason, he looked at me and said, "Buddy." There was a long pause. "If you say one more word, everybody in Neyland Stadium is gonna know about us going around." I sensed this was a good time to keep my mouth shut. I turned to Becca, rolled my eyes, and kept quiet.

Indeed, it turned out to be a safety, and five minutes later, Herschel Walker, Georgia's highly-touted freshman tailback, made the most famous run in Georgia football history, breaking two tackles and barreling over Bill Bates inside the five-yard line. Herschel scored again, and Georgia led 16–15.

Tennessee made a last-ditch effort and drove the ball inside the Georgia five with less than three minutes remaining. A field goal was certain, and Georgia appeared to be headed for defeat. But undersized linebacker Nate Taylor, the Tifton termite, put his helmet on the football, and the Dawgs recovered the ball on the Tennessee two-yard line.

As the Dawgs celebrated the fumble recovery, Neyland Stadium fell quiet except for the raucous Georgia section in the far corner. The Tennessee fan that I argued with stood up to leave. He looked me in the eye and said, "Good game," and shook my hand. I admired the class act.

Proverbs 10:14 (TLB) teaches us, "A wise man holds his tongue. Only a fool blurts everything he knows; that only leads to sorrow and trouble." I was anything but wise that evening. James 3:8 tells us that no man can tame the tongue. I didn't hold my tongue as I tried to impress Becca with my football knowledge. I blurted everything that I knew about that play in enemy territory, and it almost got me in trouble! I would have felt pretty foolish if I had been escorted out and missed one of the great Georgia comebacks in school history.

> Prayer: Lord God Almighty, I thank you for every time that the Holy Spirit helps me bite my tongue before I make a complete fool of myself. I am so grateful for your guidance. In the precious name of our Savior and Lord, amen.

Update: Georgia rode the momentum of that fumble recovery to a 12–0 record and a national championship. Becca and I attended all twelve games, and I love to tease her that I married her for good luck!

FB87:
WAIVERS

JOHN 6:37, ROMANS 3:10, EPHESIANS 4:30

The one who comes to me I will by no means cast out.

—John 6:37

The average career of an NFL player is about five years, even less for a running back. When a heralded rookie with great speed, skills, and better health competes against a veteran who has been beaten down by many NFL wars, teams will often release the veteran player and pick up the rookie.

This move is called putting the veteran on waivers. If he is fortunate, he will be picked up by another team. But eventually, the player's options will run out due to injury or low performance, and he will be forced to retire from the game he loves. Most players go this route, and it is often a sad ending to a career.

When you are saved, you become a member of God's family. Rest assured that you and I have a permanent spot on God's team for eternity and will never be placed on waivers. God will never "cast us out" (John 6:37).

In pro football, a player must be good enough to stay off waivers. In having a relationship with Christ, it has not been nor will it ever be a matter of being good enough. Because no one is good enough, not one (see Romans 3:10). But through the grace of

God, not only are we saved, but we are sealed for eternity by the Holy Spirit (Ephesians 4:30) that comes to live in us when we become Christians.

> Prayer: O Lord, it is so comforting and reassuring to know that you will never kick me off your team after I give my life to Jesus. How awesome that no matter how my day is going, I can smile about my future which is secure for eternity. In Jesus's name, amen!

FB88:
THE STEEL CURTAIN

PSALM 46:2, 62:6

Yes, he alone is my rock, rescuer, defender and fortress.
Why then should I be tense with fear when trouble comes?

—Psalm 62:6

After decades of futility, the Pittsburgh Steelers emerged during the 1970s as one of the greatest pro football dynasties ever. One reason for Pittsburgh's ascent was the development of a formidable defense, which was one of the best in the history of pro football. Many fans remember the formidable linebacking tandem of Jack Lambert and Jack Ham. However, the foundation of the defense was the Pittsburgh defensive line, which was made up of number 78, Dwight White; number 63, Ernie Holmes; number 75, Joe Greene; and number 68, L. C. Greenwood, who wore gold high-top football cleats.

The four players became extremely well-known across the country because a fan painted a life-size picture of them on a bed sheet and hung it from the mezzanine level of Three Rivers Stadium. The fan painted, "Steel Curtain," on the top of the sheet to signify the toughness and impenetrability of the foursome.

This rock-hard, four-man defensive line could symbolically represent the four attributes of the power of our incomparable mighty God. First, there is the *rock*-hard toughness that keeps the enemy from penetrating our lives. Second, there is the ability to *rescue* the team from defeat by preventing opponents from scoring. Third, there is the prowess of *defenders* that stops the opposition in its tracks. Finally, there is the mighty *fortress* of a front line that cannot be conquered.

Yes, God, and God alone, is our rock, rescuer, defender, and fortress. There is no reason to fear or be tense when troubles come (Psalm 62:6) because God is with us.

> Prayer: Father God, your mighty defense cannot be penetrated. You are indeed a mighty fortress. May I find strength in you, Lord, that will take me through this day. In the holy and precious name of our Savior, amen.

FB89:
THE NON-FUMBLE

MATTHEW 7:24-27, HEBREWS 13:5

I will liken him to a wise man who built his house on the rock.

—Matthew 7:24

Becca, the girls, and I spent the 1999 Thanksgiving weekend in Kentucky with Becca's dad. The only problem was that we would be traveling on Saturday to Livingston, Tennessee, to see her uncle during the Georgia–Georgia Tech football game. Two friends videotaped the game for me and left the VHS tapes in their respective mailboxes. All I had to do was get home without knowing the final score.

About 10:00 p.m., we pulled into Atlanta, and I never saw a Tech or Georgia flag flying on any vehicle that might give away who won the game. I drove by, picked up the tapes, and popped one in the VCR.

The game was one of the epics ever played in this storied series. Allison stayed up with me, but Becca and Jillian went to bed at halftime. *That's odd*, I thought. It turns out that they already knew who won the game!

The two teams traded one touchdown after another until there was less than a minute remaining in the game, and the score was tied 48–48. Georgia tailback Jasper Sanks burst through the line all the way down to the Tech two. By now, it was just after 1:00 a.m. First and goal on the Tech two! The Dawgs would surely either score a touchdown or take a knee and kick a game-winning field goal. Allison and I were dancing quietly in the living room, already celebrating the victory.

Unfortunately for UGA fans came one of the worst calls that you will ever see. On first down, Sanks plunged through the line. As he was tackled, his elbow hit the turf and the ball popped out. The rule in football is that the ground cannot force a fumble, so he should have been ruled down. The Tech safety picked up the ball and started running. Georgia tackled him on the ten, and finally there was a whistle!

"No!" we screamed. "No, wait, you can't do that!"

In 1999, there was no review by a replay official, so the bad call stood. Georgia lost in overtime, 51–48. I was so angry and wound up over the game that I didn't get to sleep until 3:30 a.m. I did not handle the adversity well, to say the least.

How prepared are you when a bad call or stunning upset in life happens? No one can ever be fully prepared when misfortunes strike, but instead of losing it and going into shock, cling to the One who is always there with you no matter what you're going through. God will be by your side, win or lose (Hebrews 13:5), and you can count on God to see you through the worst of times. Build your foundation upon the rock, Jesus Christ (Matthew 7:24–27). Be prepared for life's ups and downs by being committed to Christ and relying on him. Be filled with the Holy Spirit, who helps you bounce back from adversity.

> Prayer: Dear Lord, thank you for always being there for me, especially when the ball doesn't bounce my way. May I put my total trust and faith in your promises because you are always right and you never change. In the name of Jesus, amen.

FB90:
WHO DO YOU WORK FOR?

1 PETER 2:23, COLOSSIANS 3:17, 23; HEBREWS 12:2

When they hurled their insults at Him, He entrusted himself to Him who judges justly.

—1 Peter 2:23

In 2010, UGA Head Football Coach Mark Richt experienced his first losing season in eleven years at UGA after the Bulldogs lost to the University of Central Florida in a dismal showing in the Liberty Bowl. The 2010 campaign followed an 8–5 season in 2009, which came on the heels of a disappointing 10–3 season in 2008 when the Bulldogs were the preseason number one team in the nation.

Georgia lost its first two games in 2011, and Coach Richt was being skewered by disgruntled fans and members of the media across the country. Following the South Carolina loss, every game was a "must win" for Richt to keep his job. Six consecutive wins later, Coach Richt explained his approach in dealing with the onslaught of criticism and negativity.

Mark revealed his philosophy at a Tuesday press conference where he provided the following quote:

When all the games are done and all the life is lived, I know where I'll be for eternity. Not to say that I don't care what happens in this world because that's not true. Colossians 3:23 says, "Whatever you do, do your work heartily as unto the Lord," so that's what I was doing on a daily basis. I was doing my job as best I could and trying to do [it] for his glory and try[ing] not to worry about anything else.

Here is a man comfortable in his own skin because he truly knows who he works for. Even as the insults were hurled at him, Mark followed the example of Jesus and trusted his future to his real boss (no, not his wife, Kathryn!) (1 Peter 2:23). Coaching football is what he does, and he does it extremely well as proven by over one hundred ten wins in twelve years. But God is his number one priority, and family is his number two priority.

In a hostile world that threatens you from every direction, who would you say that you work for? Is it your company or the business you own? Is it the school that you were so driven to get into? Follow the example of Paul in Colossians, who wrote "Whatever you do, in word or deed, do everything in the name of the Lord Jesus Christ" (Colossians 3:17, KJV). Furthermore, work as though whatever you are doing, you are doing for Jesus Christ, our Lord and Savior, and not just for those who employ you (Colossians 3:23). With Jesus Christ as your singular focus (Hebrews 12:2), you will handle the arrows of criticism that fly at you much more effectively and serenely. Let's remember that people are watching us when adversity strikes. When we work through our problems with grace, we bring honor to Christ.

Prayer: Dear Lord, no matter how well or how poorly things are going, Coach Richt knows that ultimately he works for you. May I have that same mindset in school or in the workplace. In Jesus's name, amen.

FB91:
AMERICA'S NEXT MOST
INFLUENTIAL CHRISTIAN

PSALM 1:3, 37:23; JOHN 15:8, 2 TIMOTHY 4:2

My true disciples produce bountiful harvests. This brings
great glory to my Father.

—John 15:8 (TLB)

In October 2011, the Detroit Lions blasted the Broncos 45–10 in
Denver. Tim Tebow had a tough day and was sacked numerous
times. A Lions defensive end "Tebowed" after one sack near midfield. I mentally wrote Tebow and the Broncos off for the season.

But look what happened. The Broncos reeled off six wins in
a row to move to 8–5. Tebow led the Broncos to four improbable fourth-quarter comebacks. While many experts and fans
have challenged his quarterbacking skills, no one could rightfully
challenge his ability to lead a team back from the brink of defeat.
The eighth win featured the Chicago Bears losing a ten-point
lead with less than five minutes to play. The Bears would have
won except for a running back inexplicably going out of bounds,
which gave Denver time to kick a long field goal to tie the game
with ":00" on the clock. I don't believe that God determines the

outcome of games, but that one reminded me of the movie *Angels in the Outfield*!

The Tebow phenomenon was widespread across the country even before his first successful streak in the NFL, due in part to his visibility as a high-profile Christian athlete and Heisman Trophy winner in college. With the popularity of the NFL at an all-time high, Tebow's recognition factor was higher than any other athlete according to Brian Noe of ESPN 104.5 (Albany, NY). In our sports-obsessed society, he is one of the most popular athletes in America and is the most highly-recognized Christian in sports.

A Barna Group poll asked people to name the most influential Christian leader in America, and two out of five people did not name even one. The top vote-getter was ninety-four-year-old Dr. Billy Graham. In the not-too-distant future, Dr. Graham will receive one of the biggest welcome-home parties ever thrown in heaven. There is no clear-cut successor. Barring injury and with some degree of success in the NFL, Tebow could very well surface as the most influential Christian leader in America in this age of Facebook, blogs, and Twitter.

Tim has proven to be a dedicated worker for the kingdom with a servant's heart (John 15:8) through his mission work in the Philippines and is obviously not ashamed to express his love and gratitude for his Savior and Lord (2 Timothy 4:2) on and off the field. He exemplifies the hope in Christ that America needs so badly. Let's pray for God's protection from the enemy and strength for Tim to remain steadfast.

> Prayer: Father God, we need Christian leadership so desperately in our country. It may not look like it used to look, so help us recognize that Christian leaders can be found in our lives in many forms. In Jesus's name, amen.

FB92:
WHAT DO I DO?

PSALM 38:39, PHILIPPIANS 1:19-26, 3:12

For to me, to live is Christ, and to die is gain.

—Philippians 1:21

The month of January is when the very best undergraduate college football players decide whether to turn pro and declare for the draft of the National Football League (NFL), the ultimate level of football. Some should stay because they are simply not ready. Others should go because they will likely be taken in the first round, which is where the big money is.

It is a difficult situation for many players because they long to stay with their college teams, particularly if their teams are a threat to make a run at a conference championship and even a national championship the following year. Rest assured that these young men receive plenty of advice from their parents, guardians, family members, teammates, coaches, and friends about what route to take.

Paul acknowledged a similar dilemma. He was torn between going to heaven to be with God or continuing as a disciple of Jesus Christ to the Jews and Gentiles. Hard-pressed is a term that he used to describe his situation. Paul shared his internal struggles with the people of Philippi and chose to "press on" (see

Philippians 3:12) for the glory of God. Eventually, God called him up to the next level after he courageously endured many incredible hardships for the kingdom.

We all have friends or family members who are in poor health or face circumstances that are weighing them down. As Christians, we are called to make every effort to bring it each day and be the best we can be to honor God. God makes it possible for us to endure with the strength that only he can provide because God is our strength in time of trouble (Psalm 38:39).

> Prayer: Most gracious Father God, when I look at the difficulties that I am facing, it is no wonder that I long to be with you in a kingdom where there is no more sorrow or pain. But I know that you expect me to give my best effort until that wonderful day comes. Give me the strength, wisdom, and perseverance to live for you as Christ lives for you. In the holy name of Jesus, amen.

FB93:
COACH-IN-WAITING

DEUTERONOMY 34, JOSHUA 3:11-4:7

And it came to pass, when all the people had completely crossed over the Jordan, that the Lord spoke to Joshua.

—Joshua 4:1

College football programs often name an internal successor to the head coach for several reasons. First, the football program seeks to maintain continuity among its staff members by naming an in-house successor. Second, some rival schools will take advantage when a legendary coach is leaving by telling recruits that the football program will be weaker or without direction. Therefore, programs began naming a successor who is called a coach-in-waiting. It is understood by everyone that when the time comes, he will become the new head coach. The coach-in-waiting is often the offensive coordinator or defensive coordinator, and he is groomed for the position. The coach-in-waiting is exposed to as many situations as possible so that he will be ready to take over and maintain the winning tradition.

One of the most visible examples of a coach-in-waiting was at Florida State University. Legendary Coach Bobby Bowden handed the reins to Jimbo Fisher, who had been named the coach-in-waiting several years prior to Bowden's retirement.

Jimbo was trained under Bobby's tutelage to be ready when Bobby left coaching.

Moses laid the groundwork for the Israelis to make it to the Promised Land west of the Jordan River. After four hundred years, Israel escaped from Egypt because Moses led them through the parted waters of the Red Sea. On the day that God brought Moses up to Mount Nebo and showed Moses the land that he had promised to Abraham's descendants, he told Moses that he would not be going there with them. Moses died in the land of Moab and was buried on that side of the Jordan River.

However, Joshua had been named the "coach-in-waiting" to replace Moses. Someone had to carry the torch after Moses, and Joshua had been selected and groomed for the leadership position (see Deuteronomy 34:9). Joshua would be the person to lead the Chosen People to the other side of the Jordan River after God parted those waters (see Joshua 3:16–17).

> Prayer: Father God, any saint with a ministry or mission needs a coach-in-waiting. May each of us identify and groom the best person to continue his or her ministry for your kingdom. In Jesus's name, amen.

FB94:
TO AND FRO

2 CHRONICLES 16:9, 1 PETER 5:7

For the eyes of the Lord run to and fro.

—2 Chronicles 16:9 (KJV)

It is pretty amazing to watch a veteran NFL quarterback dissect a defense. From the shotgun formation, the QB takes the snap. Using superior vision and knowledge of defensive tendencies, he recognizes that his primary receiver is covered. In the blink of an eye, he hones in on his secondary receiver, who is also covered like a blanket. As the three-hundred-pound behemoths from the defensive line rush him like wild animals on the loose, he spots his fullback out of the backfield just in time for a ten-yard gain and another first down! The ability of the quarterback to decipher those variables and find the open man is one reason that top quarterbacks are often tagged as franchise players, which makes them among the highest paid players in the NFL.

Just as the quarterback is looking to and fro across the playing field, did you realize that God is constantly looking to and fro, checking on his loyal believers on earth, including you and me? He is constantly checking to see if we are about to be in harm's way. We are assured in 2 Chronicles 16:9 that God's eyes are running to and fro, and that God sees everything that happens to us. The New Testament assures us that he is watching everything that concerns us (see 1 Peter 5:7). He has never misread a coverage when it comes to Satan plotting against us, and he never will.

> Prayer: Most precious Lord and Savior, I thank you and our Father God that you are so concerned about us every moment. I am so grateful that you redeemed me and that you protect me as your friend and a child of God. Please continue to run your eyes to and fro so that I can be fully protected. In Jesus's name, amen.

FB95:
FOLLOWING THE SCRIPT

JEREMIAH 29:11, JOSHUA 1:9

I know the plans that I have for you, declares the Lord,
plans for welfare and not for harm, to give you a future
and a hope.

—Jeremiah 29:11 (NASB)

Football offensive coordinators will create a game plan for their
offense to execute the first ten or fifteen offensive plays of the
game in a specific order. The team practices the plays in sequence
during the week, and they will attempt to execute the plays in
that order during the game. Now, here is the stunner, which I
don't pretend to understand. There are teams that will run those
plays no matter what the score is. I suppose the coaches believe
that when they have gotten all of the plays down that they can
out-execute the opponent. But I question the soundness of the
strategy when the previous play loses eight yards to make it third
and eighteen, and the next play in the sequence is a handoff up
the middle to the fullback.

Christians who should know better, including myself, spend
an awful lot of time scripting their lives and trying to make every
move come out as happily, as risk-free, and as painlessly as possible. Even when circumstances change, they continue to bash
their heads against the wall without ever changing the plan that

they have concocted by themselves. "Going to the well" over and over just doesn't work when God is not involved in the plan.

God has an awesome plan for each of us, and we need to trust him, be obedient, and follow his plan. Here is what I learned from Ernie Johnson Jr. when he spoke at my church, Mt. Zion UMC, in Marietta, Georgia. Ernie—the studio host of the popular *NBA on TNT* show that features Charles Barkley, Kenny Smith and Shaquille O'Neal—talked about how the "unscripted life" is much more exciting and fulfilling. He had the good wife, the two kids, and the great job when Cheryl suggested that they adopt a child with special needs from Romania. Michael was followed by an adopted sister from Paraguay, and Ernie and Cheryl adopted two more children in 2011. Ernie explained that there is no telling what is coming up next in his family, but he learned to trust that God will bring them through any situation that arises. Having personally beaten non-Hodgkin's lymphoma, Ernie's conclusion is that he has learned to "trust God, period."

If I stopped worrying about what is going to happen next and stopped trying to script my game plan to be as risk-free as possible, and if instead I spent that time with God, I believe that I would be a lot closer to God and his perfect plan for my life. The Bible coaches us in 365 different verses to have no fear. That's one verse for every day of the year. Ernie reminded us that if we only trust God in the good times, in whom will we place our trust during the rocky times? Joshua reminds us to not be afraid or dismayed, for the Lord your God is with you wherever you go (see Joshua 1:9).

The deeper your faith, the less you are swayed by the unpredictable moments. The closer you are to God, you will realize much more often that he provides the mercy and grace that can only come from a perfect Father.

Prayer: Father God, please forgive me for not trusting you completely. You love me infinitely and care deeply about what happens to me because I am your child. May I turn the reins over to you and allow you to take me where you need me to go, and believe with all my heart that you will protect me and my family. In the holy name of Jesus, amen.

FB96:
THE GREATEST COMEBACK

MATTHEW 28:1-6, REVELATION 19:11-21

Then I saw heaven opened, and behold, a white horse! The one sitting on it is called Faithful and True, and in righteousness, He judges and makes war. His eyes are like a flame of fire, and on His head are many diadems, and He has a name written that no one knows but Himself.

—Revelation 19:11–12

Eli Manning emerged as the best comeback quarterback in the NFL. He led the Giants to six fourth-quarter comebacks during the 2011 season that enabled New York to finish 8–8 and make the playoffs as a wild card. Eli led the New Yorkers to easy wins over Atlanta and Green Bay and defeated San Francisco to get to the 2012 Super Bowl.

Late in the fourth quarter of Super Bowl XLV, Eli took the Giants on a ninety-two-yard drive, highlighted by one of the most incredible throws you will ever see. From the New York five-yard line, Manning threaded the needle to Mario Manningham, who caught the ball near midfield, just inches from the sideline between two New England Patriot defenders who had closed quickly. How good was the throw? Stand in your yard and throw a football through the eight-by-twelve-inch pane of glass in your neighbor's window across the street. And do it with two big barking dogs breathing down your neck! That's how good the throw was.

Manning led the Giants to the winning TD. He orchestrated an eerily similar fourth-quarter comeback in the 2008 Super Bowl against, you guessed it, the Patriots. After his 2012 Super Bowl performance, he will likely go down as the greatest comeback quarterback of his era, having done it twice on the biggest stage in sports.

Just as Eli is recognized by many as the greatest comeback QB of his time, my friend, Coach Rick Johnson, reminded me that Jesus pulled off the greatest comeback anywhere (see Matthew 28:1–6) when God raised him from the grave on the third day. Jesus is alive! While that comeback was truly amazing, there is a second comeback on the horizon that will surpass the first one. Jesus will come back for the second and final time, riding triumphantly on a white horse (see Revelation 19:11–21). That comeback will topple Satan as Christ becomes the ruler of this world.

> Prayer: Father God, thank you for the greatest comeback in history when you raised Jesus from the dead to save us from our sins, and thank you in advance for the comeback when Jesus returns to reign supreme. In Jesus's holy name, amen.

FB97:
THINGS TO COME

1 CORINTHIANS 15:50-58

Behold, I tell you a mystery: We shall not all sleep, but
we shall all be changed—in a moment, in the twinkling
of an eye, at the last trumpet. For the trumpet will sound,
and the dead will be raised incorruptible, and we shall be
changed.

—1 Corinthians 15:51–52

In the Southeastern Conference, the spring football game has
become increasingly popular. In the 1970s and 1980s, teams
would play their spring games before several thousand fans. As
the popularity of SEC football increased after SEC teams won a
number of consecutive national championships, it became com-
monplace for forty to fifty thousand fans to attend. Some will
come to the game just so they can have a bigger crowd than their
rival teams. The signing of Nick Saban as head coach of Alabama
was such big news that ninety-two thousand fans showed up in
Tuscaloosa for his first spring game.

The actual spring games are not so entertaining. It's typi-
cally a laidback atmosphere, and there are special rules to prevent injuries. The quarterbacks wear green jerseys to keep from
being injured, and there is no rushing the punter or kicker on
field goal attempts.

But the excitement for the fans comes from seeing the new offensive and defensive prospects for the upcoming fall. Does the highly touted redshirt freshman running back get to the hole quick enough? How does the new 3–4 defense look? These fans are hungry for a foretaste of things to come in the fall. They're hoping that the outlook is promising. But often their grandiose expectations are tempered by an injury to a key player, or perhaps that running back is actually a step slower than touted.

As Christians, this life on earth is but a glimpse of the glory to come. We look at the blessings that God puts in front of us today and can never fully imagine how much sweeter heaven will be. When we attempt to take a grandiose look at heaven, we always fall short. We look longingly from the "spring game" when we get a glimpse of the great things to come, to the "fall season" when one day we see the majesty of heaven played out for eternity. We look forward to donning our brand new, immortal, incorruptible, and resurrected bodies (see 1 Corinthians 15:50–58) after the last trumpet sounds.

> Prayer: Father God, thank you for the glimpses of the great things to come that you give me as a follower of Christ. When I try to imagine how much better and more beautiful heaven will be, I fall short every time. I long for the day when I bow before you with the utmost awe and respect. In the name of Jesus who made it all possible, amen.

FB98:
UNLEASHING YOUR
SPIRITUAL GIFTS

ROMANS 12:4-8, 1 CORINTHIANS 2:9, 12:4-6

Let us use them.

—Romans 12:6

On July 14, 2012, our daughter Allison, a staunch Georgia Bulldogs fan, married Kevin, who loves the Alabama Crimson Tide, in Atlanta. Allison was such a beautiful bride, the wedding ceremony was very touching, and the reception was replete with great food and a band that had people dancing until the end! Jillian gave a heartfelt speech for her sister and even threw in a "Roll Tide!" for her new brother-in-law.

Before the newlyweds walked to the limo, crimson-and-white football shakers were given to the Alabama fans and red-and-black shakers went to the UGA fans. An Auburn fan was a good sport and took one of each. Each fan base lined one side of the stairway shouting, "Roll Tide!" then "Go Dawgs!" Our friends Franklin and Elizabeth stood on the Georgia side. Franklin's family has had Georgia season tickets for years, and he and I have chatted many times about the Dawgs. He wore his oval *G*

Georgia pin on his suit lapel that evening. Franklin was laid back at the reception until the Bama fans ignited his passion!

At the top of the stairs, Kevin's friend Daniel suddenly yelled, "Rammer jammer yellow hammer!" The Bama fans then yelled, "We're gonna beat the h—— out of you!" Several Rammer Jammers shook their shakers in the direction of the Georgia fans, which fired up Franklin. He wasn't about to be outdone on his home turf! For the next Georgia cheer, Franklin waved his shaker furiously and yelled at the top of his lungs, "Go Dawgs! Sic 'em! Woof! Woof! Woof!" He waved his shaker in such a big circle that he hit me in the head. *Thwack! Thwack!* I leaned backward to keep from getting pummeled!

Franklin's passion for the Dawgs had clearly been awakened. When was the last time your passion for Christ was ignited? Chip Ingram in *The Devine Design* wrote that God gives each Christian one or more spiritual gifts (see Romans 12:4–8 and 1 Corinthians 12 to learn more). The sad thing is that many spiritual gifts lie dormant for a long period of time. Some are never used.

The joy in a Christian's life is amplified when a person discovers how to unleash his or her spiritual gifts (Romans 12:6) for God. My spiritual gift was leading the youth basketball ministry at Mt. Zion UMC, and I later discovered writing sports devotions was a gift. Your gift could be teaching Sunday school, feeding the homeless, making music, building a Home for Habitat, writing encouraging notes, leading a ministry at your church, or coaching a youth team. There is at least one special gift within every Christian, and the Holy Spirit can spur you to use it and help God grow your local church and his kingdom.

Haven't found your spiritual gift yet? If not, keep searching the Scriptures daily, meeting with God in prayer, and speaking with your Christian brothers and sisters. During your quiet time, consider the activities that make you light up. God will lead you to your spiritual gift in his perfect time if you seek his face (2 Chronicles 7:14) and strive for obedience. He will show you where he is working, and he will give you the power to use your special gift in ways that you would have never dreamed (1 Corinthians 2:9).

> Prayer: Most gracious and giving Father, thank you for the spiritual gifts that you give believers. May I unleash my spiritual gifts with enthusiasm and passion so that my light burns brightly for Christ. In the precious name of our Lord Jesus, amen.

FB99:
WRONG WAY!

ISAIAH 30:21, JOHN 14:6

I am the Way, the Truth and the Life.

—John 14:6

Becca, Jillian, and I attended the 2011 Georgia–Vanderbilt game in Nashville. UGA defensive end Ray Drew forced a fumble by the quarterback on the last play of the first half. He picked up the fumble and ran several yards before he was tackled by two Vandy linemen. But the problem was that Drew was running the wrong way toward his goal line. Several teammates were in position to stop him had the linemen missed Drew, who incidentally became an ordained preacher at the age of seventeen.

The play reminded me of Jim "Wrong Way" Marshall of the Purple People Eaters defensive unit of the Minnesota Vikings. Along with fellow Hall of Famers Carl Eller and Alan Page, Marshall made up one-fourth of one of the greatest defensive lines in pro football history. In a game at Kezar Stadium in San Francisco, a 49er fumbled near the Viking thirty-yard line. Marshall swooped in, picked up the fumble, and raced for the goal line. The wrong goal line. His teammates tried in vain to catch him from behind, but he crossed the Viking goal line and tossed the ball high in the air. A 49er lineman thanked him for handing his team a safety on the play.

Look at your life. Are you going the wrong way? It's easy to get caught running the wrong way, but there is only one correct way. That way is Jesus Christ, who proclaimed that "I am the Way, the Truth, and the Life. No one comes to the Father except through Me" (John 14:6). Not a way. Not one way. *The* way. The *only* way. Jesus is the only way to God, to salvation, and eternal life in heaven. Won't you run to the Savior now?

> Prayer: Dear Lord, your gospel is so simple to remember. Jesus is the Way. He is the Truth. He is the Life. Without Jesus, I have no chance. With Jesus, I have the only chance that I will ever need. Thank you for the Savior of the world! In Jesus's name, amen.

FB100:
HELMET STICKERS

REVELATION 2

And I will give to each one of you according to your works.

—Revelation 2:23

Remember the gold stars that you earned as an elementary student for good grades and helping the teacher? ESPN aired a story about the clever use of helmet stickers in college football. One of the first schools to use stickers was Miami of Ohio in the early 1960s. Fifty years later, college players are very particular about receiving stickers for good plays. Each week, twenty-two FBS schools award helmet stickers for outstanding plays. The University of Georgia awards white dog bones for good football plays and black dog bones for academic achievement. Vanderbilt awards anchors in line with its Commodore nickname. Each Saturday night, the ESPN staff gives helmet stickers to the players with the most outstanding games of the day.

Only by repenting of our sin and accepting God's free gift of grace will we ever enter heaven. But God will award us in heaven for our earthly good deeds in the name of Jesus Christ. The awards will be in the form of a crown that is adorned in a way that measures up to our contributions to the kingdom. The number and types of awards will be exactly suited to us. They will vary from person to person. In heaven, we will agree exactly with what God has awarded each person, and there will be no jealousy.

There are opportunities all around us to share his love. What will you do to earn a helmet sticker from the Lord?

> Prayer: Dear Lord, I look forward to seeing the fancy helmet stickers that you will have for me in heaven. I realize that I don't get all of them now because I would think it's all about me instead of you. I will wait patiently for your rewards and give you the glory in the meantime. In the name of your Son who went to the cross for me, amen.

FB101: CALLED OUT

PSALM 19:12, 34:14, 51:10; ISAIAH 50:4, 1 JOHN 1:7-9

Turn from all known sin and spend your time doing good.
Try to live in peace with everyone, work hard at it.

—Psalm 34:14 (TLB)

The 2012 University of Georgia defensive unit was touted by some experts during August as the best in the nation. However, the Georgia D was mostly ineffective during the first six games, giving up forty-four points to Tennessee and thirty-five to South Carolina. Despite the Georgia D's decline, NFL experts continued to project that up to four UGA defensive players would be selected in the first round of the next draft. Clearly chemistry was lacking.

Following Georgia's lackluster 29–24 win over Kentucky, senior safety Shawn Williams let his teammates have it full bore. Speaking to a reporter, Williams "called out" his teammates for playing with a lack of enthusiasm and passion. His anger and frustration were evident as he pleaded with his teammates to give maximum effort and "man up." His emotional words spread through the blog grapevine like wildfire. Several teammates initially took strong exception to his words that cut like a knife, but later they acknowledged that the Georgia D indeed needed to "recommit to the D." The increased commitment was evident in the next game against Florida as the emotionally-charged Bulldogs defense forced six turnovers and defeated the Gators 17–9. The defense followed the Florida victory with three impressive performances, and their second-half season defensive stats were on par with the 2011 season.

Neither his head coach nor his defensive coordinator was able to achieve what Shawn did. Perhaps his teammates respected him and responded because "Shawn called us out." Though he did it in an unusual way, his plea exemplified deep caring, commitment, and leadership. Shawn helped his unit come together, dig deeper, and raise their play to a much higher level. The consensus opinion in the Bulldog Nation was that Shawn's heartfelt plea turned the season around and allowed Georgia to control their destiny in its quest for the national championship.

When you and I dip well below the performance standards that Christ taught us, God calls us out to repent through the leading of the Holy Spirit. That leading can occur through everyday circumstances, during prayer, while reading Scripture, and often during an interaction with a friend, family member, or colleague. Long, long ago, God chose to grow his kingdom by using his flawed people. He uses someone to help turn us from our sinful ways so we can positively impact other people.

The message to repent has fallen on many deaf ears and hardened hearts throughout the centuries. Upon the command of our loving God, the major and minor prophets repeatedly "called out" the Israelites, his chosen ones who continued to worship false gods and follow their evil ways. Today, pastors give us wise counsel, call us to obedience, and inspire us to achieve great things for the kingdom of God. However, because so many people are not part of a Christian faith community, we need to encourage these people, who are our friends and colleagues. But to be effective, we've got to be right with God.

Psalm 34:14 (TLB) reads, "Turn from all known sin and spend your time doing good. Try to live in peace with everyone, work hard at it." Examine your activities over the past few weeks. You may discover that you have fallen into disobedience in a certain part of your life. Ask God to set you free and restore you fully to him. "Create in me a clean heart, O God, and renew a right spirit within me" (Psalm 51:10).

When we are in sync with God, the light of Christ shines brightly through us, and that light cannot be hidden (see Matthew 5:15). Through our Christ-like lifestyle, God can use us to call out others, but that doesn't mean verbal chastisement in a holier-than-thou way. When we don't put others down because they are different, when we don't participate in questionable activities, or when we send someone a caring text or card at just the right time, God can use our actions to open the eyes of others to his perfect love. Hopefully, others will see Christ's love in us instead of seeing imperfect Christians.

> Prayer: Father God, often I underestimate the influence that I can have on the people I love. Help me live in a way that shines your light and calls out the need for others to turn to you. Thank you for the love, hope, peace, and eternal life made possible by our Lord and Savior's sacrifice at Calvary. In the name of the Lord Jesus Christ, amen.

INDEX

VERSES

3:23		FB90
	Daniel	
3:12–25		FB63
9:24–27		FB44
9:25		FB09
	Deuteronomy	
34		FB93
	Ephesians	
2:8–9		FB81
4:30		FB36, FB77, FB81, FB87
	Exodus	
17:11–14		FB54
20:1–17		FB03
20:3		FB73
	Ezekiel	
36:24–27		FB85
36:26		FB23
	Galatians	
4:4		FB09
5:22–23		FB56, FB66
	Genesis	
3:13		FB72
39:7–21		FB15
	Hebrews	
4:16		FB21
10:10		FB70

12:2	FB90
13:1–5	FB66
13:5	FB52, FB74, FB84, FB89
13:8	FB74, FB84

Isaiah

7:14	FB14
9:6	FB14
28:16	FB69
30:21	FB99
42:8	FB37
44:6	FB37
44:8	FB37
45:5	FB13, FB37, FB73
45:22	FB13, FB32, FB37
50:4	FB101
55:8–9	FB25

James

1	FB72
1:2–4	FB42
2:17	FB49
3:1–8	FB86
4:14–15	FB11

Jeremiah

1:5–6	FB23
17:5–8	FB60
29:11	FB27, FB60, FB95

Job

1:13–2:10	FB38

John

3:16	FB04, FB42
3:16–17	FB50, FB59
3:17	FB59
3:30	FB39, FB73
4:7–26	FB04
6:37	FB77, FB87
6:38	FB80
6:44	FB24
8:6–11	FB68
10:10	FB22
14:2–4	FB46
14:6	FB99
15:5	FB30
15:8	FB91
15:12	FB01
16:33	FB51
18:3–11	FB58
20:25–29	FB61
21:19	FB60

Joshua

1:8	FB17

Luke

2:10–16	FB14, FB45
2:42–49	FB80

3:21–22		FB36
9:23		FB82
15:3–10		FB65
15:10		FB06
	Mark	
12:30–31		FB01
	Matthew	
3:1		FB23
4:17		FB23
5:23–28		FB15
6:25–33		FB83
6:30		FB24
6:33		FB41
7:7		FB17, FB22
7:13		FB33
7:24–27		FB05, FB89
11:28		FB40
16:13–16		FB70
16:26		FB73
21:42		FB69
25:40		FB01
26:36–44		FB08, FB79
26:69–75		FB74
27:26		FB79
27:31–33		FB79
27:32		FB41
27:32–50		FB01, FB79

27:38–43		FB44
27:51		FB21
28:1–6		FB79, FB96
	Micah	
5:2		FB14
	Nehemiah	
2:5		FB09
	Numbers	
14:18		FB66
	Philippians	
1:6		FB19, FB31, FB53
1:19–26		FB92
1:20–21		FB42
2:8–11		FB35
2:12–16		FB75
2:17		FB48, FB64
3:8		FB42
3:11–14		FB07, FB67
3:12		FB92
3:14		FB10
4:12		FB48, FB64
4:13		FB26
4:19		FB17
	Proverbs	
3:5–6		FB29, FB83
10:31–32		FB86
18:24		FB74, FB84

Psalms

1:3	FB91
7:11–13	FB18
12:6–7	FB12
18:29	FB51
19:12	FB101
34:14	FB101
37:4	FB28
37:23	FB91
38:39	FB92
46:1	FB63
46:2	FB88
51:10	FB101
62:6	FB88
62:6–7	FB05
119:100–105	FB52
119:105	FB52
139:1–14	FB47
139:23–24	FB78

Revelation

1:8–13	FB20
2	FB100
3:20	FB02
5:11	FB06
19:11–21	FB96
20:11–21:5	FB43
21:1–5	FB16

Romans	
2:1–16	FB18
3:10	FB87
3:23	FB13, FB84
6:23	FB81
7:14–25	FB78
8:18	FB16, FB34
8:26–39	FB76
8:28	FB06
12:2	FB04
12:4–8	FB98
Titus	
3:5	FB02
Zephaniah	
3:17	FB39

NAMES AND TERMS

A

abandonment	FB45
adversity	FB51
Alexander, Shaun	FB28
Allen, George	FB36
angels	FB01, FB06
Arnold, Amp	FB51
attitude, positive	FB61, FB64

B

Barkley, Charles	FB95
Bates, Bill	FB04
Bates, Bill	FB86
Bazemore, Wright	FB14
Belue, Buck	FB51
Bible, promises of the	FB52
Bible, Truth of the	FB12
blessings	FB22, FB28, FB41
Bowden, Bobby	FB30, FB32, FB93
Bowden, Tommy	FB32
Brees, Drew	FB48, FB49
Bullock, Sandra	FB08
Burt, Jim	FB36
Butler, Drew	FB41
Butler, Kevin	FB41

C

D

E

REFERENCES

FB04   Sports Illustrated, *More Than Georgia on His Mind*, Curry Kirkpatrick, August 31, 1981

FB07   *Me and Julio Down by the Schoolyard*, Paul Simon, 1972

FB12   *The Journey*, Billy Graham, p. 54

FB14   *Christian Examiner, Heisman Winner Has Priorities in Order*, Joni B. Hannagan, January 2008

FB15   *Forrest Gump the Movie*, 1994, Director: Robert Zemeckis, Created by Winston Groom

FB20   *Aggie Bonfire*, wikipedia.com

FB26   *fca.org, Life's Playbook, The Personal Testimony of Tony Dungy*

FB26   http://www.cbn.com/700club/features/TonyDungy_AllProDad_0610.aspx, *Tony Dungy, the All Pro Dad*, CBN Sports, by Shawn Brown

FB27   *http://www.uga.edu/teamunited/testimonies/mark_richt.htm, Mark Richt–UGA Football Head Coach*

FB27   http://www.familyfirst.net/press-room/press-releases/all-pro- dad-press-releases/tony-dungy-and-mark-richt-put-father- hood-first/, *Tony Dungy and Mark Richt Put Fatherhood First*

FB28   *Sharing the Victory Magazine*, Fellowship of Christian Athletes, December 2002

FB29   *savannahnow.com, When Herschel Walker Speaks People Listen*, Tim Guidera, October 10, 2006

FB30   *BPSports.net, Football and Faith Are Big Business for Bobby Bowden*, Sandra Vidak, June 12, 2001

FB32 *A Simple Call*, Tommy Bowden, 1973

FB36 *How Did the Tradition of Pouring Gatorade on the Winning Coach Get Started?*, http://ajc.com, January 3, 2010

FB36 *Can a Gatorade Bath Result in You Taking a Bath in Court?*, http://Collegesportsbusinessnews.com/june-2011/article/can-a-gatorade-bath-result-in-you-taking-a-bath-in-court, Joshua D. Winneker, April 25, 2011

FB38 Colt McCoy Interview with Lisa Salters of ABC-TV, http://youtube.com/watch?v=rVsSvx3UQOY, January 7, 2010

FB39 *The Mystery and Meaning of Christian Conversion*. Dr. George Morris, p. 167

FB41 *Who Am I*, Casting Crowns, 2003

FB49 *Manning*, John Underwood, p. 363

FB49 *True Saint* by Jill Ewert, Sharing the Victory Magazine, Jan/Feb 2010

FB49 *The Choice Is Clear*, February 2, 2010 by Rick Reilly, ESPN \ The Magazine

FB53 Terry Bradshaw, http://wikipedia.com

FB60 *This Day with the Master*, Dennis Kinlaw, 2002, p. 180

FB65 http://www.youtube.com/watch?v=ECL9hNEuHm0

FB68 *Michael Vick Shares First-Ever Testimony*, February 8, 2010, Baptist Press, Art Stricklin

FB69 *The Showroom*, http://www.youtube.comwatch?v=rZW5s0NY8_U, 2010

FB70 *The Case for Christ*, Lee Strobel, 1998

FB73 *Fever Pitch*, Directors Peter Farrelly and Robert Farrelly, Writer Nick Hornby, 2005

FB73 *God and Football*, Chad Gibbs, 2010

FB76 *Why are NFL quarterbacks wearing a green dot on their football helmet?*, http://hotstuff.linkpress.info/why-are-nfl-quarterbacks-wearing-a-green-dot-on-their-helmet/

FB77 *Oversigning: Arkansas Cuts to the Chase on Cutting the Fat*, http://rivals.yahoo.com/ncaa/football/blog/drsaturday/post/Oversigning-Arkansas-cuts-to-the-chase-on-cutti?urn=ncaaf-wp1658, *Matt Hinton,* May 18, 2011

FB90   *Win Streak Shows Dogs Haven't Quit Season or Richt,* http://blogs.ajc.com/jeff-schultz-blog/2011/11/08/win-streak-shows-dogs-havent-quit-on-season-or-richt/?cp=3, Jeff Schultz, November 8, 2011

FB91   *Tim Tebow Is the Most Popular Athlete in Sports,* Brian Noe, ESPN 104.5 (Albany, NY), December 8, 2011

FB91   *Billy Graham Tops List of Christian Leaders,* http://www.newsmax.com/InsideCover/graham-obama-poll-christian/2011/11/21/id/418773, Paul Scicchitano, November 21, 2011